Expectations
for the
Catholic
School
Principal

Expectations for the Catholic School Principal

◆◆◆◆◆◆◆◆◆◆◆◆◆◆

A Handbook for Pastors and Parish School Committees

Maria J. Ciriello, OP, Ph.D., Editor
Associate Professor of Education
The Catholic University of America

United States
Catholic Conference
Washington, D.C.

In its planning document, as approved by the general membership of the United States Catholic Conference in November 1992, the Department of Education was authorized to prepare materials to assist in training new principals for Catholic elementary and secondary schools to enable them to ". . . continue to provide high quality education for all their students in a context infused with gospel values." This volume, *Expectations for the Catholic School Principal: A Handbook for Pastors and Parish School Committees*, is a complementary resource to *Formation and Development of Catholic School Leaders: A Three-Volume Preparation Program for Future and Neophyte Principals* and is intended to assist in attaining this goal as outlined in the bishops' statement *In Support of Catholic Elementary and Secondary Schools*, which was issued in November 1990. This volume is approved by Most Reverend Robert J. Banks, chairman of the Committee on Education, and is authorized for publication by the undersigned.

Monsignor Dennis M. Schnurr
General Secretary
NCCB/USCC

ISBN 1-57455-054-3

Contents

◆◆◆

Foreword

This book was developed in response to requests by Catholic school superintendents and principals who expressed a need for a publication to help pastors and
parish school committees learn about the scope of responsibilities entailed in the
work of the Catholic school principal. As the numbers of religious sisters and
brothers continue to decrease in educational ministries, it is becoming the norm
for dioceses to work with pastors and a school committee to conduct a professional
search process to recruit and select the school principal. This book is intended as
a resource to acquaint pastors and school committee members with the various
roles and responsibilities intrinsic to the work of the principal.

This book is a complementary resource to *Formation and Development for Catholic
School Leaders: A Preparation Program for Future and Neophyte Principals,* a series that
provides a training curriculum for persons interested in becoming Catholic school
principals. This three-volume series is produced through the collaborative efforts
of the United States Catholic Conference and the National Catholic Educational
Association.

This volume includes the nine chapters from that series which address each of the
nine areas of leadership responsibility of a Catholic school principal. In addition,
to place the position of the Catholic school principal into a parish and diocesan
context, two new chapters were added. Monsignor Francis X. Barrett presents
some guidelines for the pastor who has a parish school. Father John A. Thomas
describes the relationship of the superintendent to the pastor and the parish school.

Along with the authors of the individual chapters, Sister Lourdes Sheehan, RSM,
the former Secretary for Education at the United States Catholic Conference,
deserves special thanks for supporting the idea of producing this book.

Maria Ciriello, OP, Ph.D., *Editor*
Associate Professor of Education
The Catholic University of America

Introduction

♦♦♦

> *The Catholic school is an evangelizing,*
> *educational community.*
>
> —*National Congress:*
> *Catholic Schools for the 21st Century:*
> *Executive Summary*, 1992, p. 17.

The expectations of Catholic school principals flow from the dual mission of Catholic schools and are shaped by its organization. The *National Congress: Catholic Schools for the 21st Century: Executive Summary* stated succinctly the belief that "Catholic schools are called to be exemplary models of academic excellence and faith development" (p. 21). Since Catholic schools provide both an academic and a religious education, the principal is expected to supply both educational and spiritual leadership. The administration of Catholic schools is ordinarily site-based. Responsibilities for decisions regarding finance, personnel, and curriculum are made at the local level. Such accountability calls for managerial leadership from the Catholic school principal.

The uniqueness of the role of the Catholic school principal lies in the responsibility to be the spiritual leader of the school. "Leadership in and on behalf of Catholic schools is deeply spiritual, servant-like, prophetic, visionary and empowering" (*National Congress* 1992, p. 29). In this capacity the principal promotes and shapes the Catholic identity of the school and motivates the staff to be faithful to the basic mission of the school: the integration of religious truth and values with life (*The Religious Dimension of Education in a Catholic School* 1988).

"The Catholic school is a unique faith-centered community which integrates thinking and believing in ways that encourage intellectual growth, nurture faith and inspire action" (*National Congress* 1992, p. 17). As spiritual leader the principal is attuned to issues of faith development, building Christian community, and moral and ethical formation as they are lived within the context of the history and philosophy of Catholic schools.

The principal of the Catholic school shares with the public school administrator the responsibility to be the educational leader of the school, but there are definite differences in the nuances of this role. As educational leader the principal is expected to promote the mission of the school through principles of good leadership and to attend to the curricular and instructional aspects of the school. Two statements from the *National Congress* (1992, p. 18) summarize the Catholic identity of the school and provide direction to the principal:

 🙢 We commit ourselves to teach an integrated curriculum rooted in gospel values and Catholic teachings.

 🙢 We welcome and support a diverse cultural and economic population as a hallmark of our Catholic identity.

Since the *raison d'etre* of the Catholic school revolves around its religious mission, the goal of the Catholic school is to have a well-rounded curriculum that addresses the emotional, spiritual, and moral development of students along with their intellectual, physical, and social growth. The curriculum becomes inclusive and universal, that is, Catholic, when the educational leader motivates the faculty to provide for all children—regardless of their ethnic, cultural, religious, or learning differences—a curriculum that reflects current knowledge and sound teaching strategies, and challenges student potential.

The managerial leadership of the Catholic school principal is wide ranging due to the autonomous way in which most parish schools are administered. The managerial responsibilities include recruiting, interviewing, selecting, orienting, and supervising the human resources of the school. In addition the principal is expected to direct the institution in an orderly and organized way and to foster institutional linkages with the parish, diocese, state, and local school districts. To ensure the future of the school, Catholic school management requires skillful application of financial, public relations, marketing and development, and long-range planning strategies.

Taken from competencies developed for Catholic school principals and presented in detail in the *Formation and Development for Catholic School Leaders: A Preparation Program for Future and Neophyte Principals* series, the following list presents in more detail the expectations for Catholic school principals.

Role: The Principal as *Spiritual Leader*

Area of responsibility: *Faith Development*

F1. Nurtures the faith development of faculty and staff through opportunities for spiritual growth
F2. Ensures quality Catholic religious instruction of students
F3. Provides opportunities for the school community to celebrate faith
F4. Supports and fosters consistent practices of Christian service

Area of responsibility: *Building Christian Community*

B1. Fosters collaboration between the parish(es) and the school
B2. Recognizes, respects, and facilitates the role of parents as primary educators
B3. Promotes Catholic community

Area of responsibility: *Moral and Ethical Development*

M1. Facilitates the moral development and maturity of children, youth, and adults
M2. Integrates gospel values and Christian ethics into the curriculum, policies, and life of the school

Area of responsibility: *History and Philosophy*

H1. Knows the history and purpose of Catholic schools in the United States
H2. Utilizes church documents and Catholic guidelines and directives
H3. Develops and implements statements of school philosophy and mission that reflect the unique Catholic character of the school

Role: The Principal as *Educational Leader*

Area of responsibility: *Leadership*

L1. Demonstrates symbolic and cultural leadership skills in developing a school climate reflecting Catholic identity
L2. Applies a Catholic educational vision to the daily activities of the school
L3. Promotes healthy staff morale
L4. Recognizes and fosters leadership ability among staff members
L5. Interprets and uses research to guide action plans
L6. Identifies and effects needed change
L7. Attends to personal growth and professional development

Area of responsibility: *Curriculum and Instruction*

C1. Demonstrates a knowledge of the content and the methods of religious education
C2. Knows of the developmental stages of children and youth
C3. Recognizes and provides for cultural and religious differences
C4. Provides leadership in curriculum development, especially for the integration of Christian values

C5. Demonstrates an understanding of a variety of educational and pedagogical skills

C6. Recognizes and accommodates the special learning needs of children within the inclusive classroom

C7. Supervises instruction effectively

C8. Demonstrates an understanding of effective procedures for evaluating the learning of students

C9. Demonstrates the ability to evaluate the general effectiveness of the learning program of the school

ROLE: PRINCIPAL AS *MANAGERIAL LEADER*

Area of responsibility: *Personnel Management*

P1. Recruits, interviews, selects, and provides an orientation for school staff

P2. Knows and applies principles of adult learning and motivation

P3. Knows and applies the skills of organizational management, delegation of responsibilities, and communication skills

P4. Uses group process skills effectively with various school committees

P5. Manages conflicts effectively

P6. Evaluates staff

Area of responsibility: *Institutional Management*

I1. Provides for an orderly school environment and promotes student self-discipline

I2. Understands Catholic school governance structures and works effectively with school boards

I3. Recognizes the importance of the relationship between the school and the diocesan office

I4. Recognizes the importance of the relationship between the school and religious congregation(s)

I5. Knows civil and canon law as it applies to Catholic schools

I6. Understands state requirements and government-funded programs

I7. Understands the usefulness of current technologies

Area of responsibility: *Finance and Development*

D1. Demonstrates skills in planning and managing the school's financial resources toward developing and monitoring an annual budget

D2. Understands the basic strategies of long-range planning and applies them in developing plans for the school

D3. Provides for development in the broadest sense, including effective public relations programs (parish[es], church, and broader community) and a school marketing program

D4. Seeks resources and support beyond the school (and parish[es])

The Principal as
SPIRITUAL
LEADER
♦♦♦

Overview

The "heart" of Catholic school leadership lies in effective spiritual leadership. Nouwen (1989) sets the tone for leadership in Catholic schools. He notes that "the leadership about which Jesus speaks is of a radically different kind from the leadership offered by the world. It is a servant leadership—to use Robert Greenleaf's term—in which the leader is a servant who needs people as much as they need him or her" (pp. 44–45). The *National Congress: Catholic Schools for the 21st Century: Executive Summary* (1992) expresses a similar sentiment: "Leadership in and on behalf of Catholic schools is rooted in an ongoing relationship with Jesus Christ and involves a shift from vertical models to collegial models" (p. 29).

The *National Congress* states definitive beliefs relating to the spiritual leadership responsibilities of the principal:

ﻉ❧ The Catholic school is an integral part of the church's mission to proclaim the Gospel, build faith communities, celebrate through worship, and serve others (p. 17).

ﻉ❧ The spiritual formation of the entire school community is an essential dimension of the Catholic school's mission (p. 17).

Four areas of responsibility are particularly pertinent to the spiritual leadership of the Catholic school principal. The first is to nurture the faith development of all who are involved with the school, including faculty, students, and parents. The second responsibility is to build Christian community and promote the values consistent with community among faculty, students, parents, parish, and local community. The third responsibility is to attend to the moral and ethical development of the students and adults of the school community. The fourth area of responsibility is to know the history and philosophy of Catholic schools, utilizing the church documents and directives as guiding principles that affect all aspects of the school program.

FAITH DEVELOPMENT

The need for effective leadership of Catholic schools is evident, especially in a fast-changing and highly competitive world. Strong leaders who believe in and are able to articulate the mission and purpose of Catholic education and who are unafraid to make the necessary decisive choices to build a future are called for in today's society (Bernardin 1989).

A Catholic school principal is expected to give continual care and attention to the religious purposes of the school by nurturing the faith life of the school community. In their 1979 pastoral message on Catholic education, *Sharing the Light of Faith,* the National Conference of Catholic Bishops reaffirmed previous messages concerning Catholic education: "It is also widely recognized that Catholic schools are to be communities of faith in which the Christian message, the experience of community, worship, and social concern are integrated in the total experience of students, their parents, and members of the faculty" (no. 9).

In order to nurture the faith development of faculty and staff, the principal as spiritual leader is expected to provide them opportunities for spiritual growth. Focusing on the students, the principal will ensure that their religious instruction is systematic, current, comprehensive, and appropriately conveyed. Finally, the principal will coordinate opportunities for the school community to celebrate the faith together and to render Christian service to one another, the parish, and the civic community.

In *Nurturing Faith: The Principal's Trust,* Muccigrosso (page 5) contends that the Catholic school principal is called to be a transformational leader of the school community. When principals facilitate the faith development of the school community, they are fostering a mission-oriented central identity for the school.

BUILDING CHRISTIAN COMMUNITY

The school community, as an educational institution, necessarily has a life of its own. But a Catholic school is also a community within a wider community. Traditionally and by design, it maintains a family-school-parish interaction. (*Sharing the Light of Faith* 1979, no. 232). As a result of Vatican II, a new awareness of the importance of community continues to unfold as the Church, describing itself as the People of God, carries out its mission (*The Religious Dimension of Education in a Catholic School* 1988, no. 31).

To foster the building of community, the principal is expected to foster collaboration in team ministry to promote a variety of gifts of the Spirit, to encourage parents to respond to their important role as the primary educators of their children, and to promote Catholic community. Such activities will enable the principal to lead the school in the important mission of reflecting Christ's attitude to all who attend and are associated with the school.

Curran's reflections on *Christian Community: The Principal's Challenge* (page 14) highlight the pivotal role of the principal's personal spiritual development in successfully fostering a spirit of school community. He challenges leaders to nurture a vision that unites the school community to work together.

MORAL AND ETHICAL DEVELOPMENT

As a caring institution with a covenant-like relationship, the school accepts its responsibility to do everything it can to care for the full range of the needs of its students, teachers, and administrators. Beyond intellectual values, an important task of the Catholic school is that of "developing persons who are responsible and inner-directed, capable of choosing freely in conformity with their consciences." Moreover, moral and ethical principles are individually and corporately adhered to as an outlook on life that permeates the school (*The Catholic School* 1977, nos. 31, 32).

The principal as spiritual leader in a Catholic school is expected to be able to facilitate the moral development and maturity of children, youth, and adults. Integrating gospel values and Christian ethics into the curriculum, policies, and life of the school is another way the principal demonstrates spiritual leadership. Attention given by the Catholic school principal to the integration of Christian values in what is being taught, as well as the exemplification of these values in decisions and actions, will aid in forming a moral community with a value system rooted in the Gospels.

Moral and ethical formation are central to the purpose of Catholic schools. Considering the current problems of society as a context, Muccigrosso in *Moral and Ethical Development: The Principal's Charge* (page 23) demonstrates the critical need principals address when they attend to the moral and ethical development of those involved with the school.

HISTORY AND PHILOSOPHY

As Catholic educators approach the twenty-first century, they are being challenged to clearly identify the aims of Catholic education. Heft (1991) proposes that a review of the history of the Catholic school in the United States is necessary to understand why the Catholic school system was formed, to be confident of its success, and to envision ways of adapting this legacy to the needs of today.

In the teaching ministry, one is privileged to fulfill a special role within the Church and within society. Guidance for the task, which includes transmitting clearly the message of salvation, can be found in many documents and directives of the Church (*The Catholic School of the '80s* 1987).

The principal as spiritual leader in a Catholic school is expected to know the history and purpose of Catholic schools in the United States. The principal will utilize church documents and Catholic guidelines and directives to develop and implement statements of school philosophy and mission that reflect the unique Catholic character of the school.

Kealey presents in *History and Philosophy: The Principal's Foundation* (page 33), a chronological account of decisive events that have indelibly influenced the progress and philosophy of Catholic schools. Being aware of the roots and guiding principles of Catholic education arms the principal with knowledge and understanding that provide purposeful direction to the school.

Nurturing Faith:
The Principal's Trust

Robert Muccigrosso, Ph.D.

The mandate undertaken by the Catholic school is to be transformational in the fullest sense of that word:

> ... the [Catholic school] is educating its students to promote effectively the welfare of the earthly city, and preparing them to serve the advancement of the reign of God. The purpose in view is that by living an exemplary and apostolic life, the Catholic graduate can become ... the saving leaven of the human family (*Declaration on Christian Education* 1966, no. 7).

Likewise leadership is called to be transformational (Burns 1978, Covey 1991, De Pree 1992, Ramsey 1991). Bernardin (1989) cites the talent for visionary leadership to be essential to Catholic education. He calls the principal to be a risk taker who clearly and emphatically speaks about the mission and purpose of Catholic education. Building upon the solid foundation provided by the requisite educational and managerial expertise, the Catholic school principal is challenged to the critical task of fostering the spiritual and faith development of all who comprise the Catholic school community: students and staff and parents when possible.

> Catholic schools are to be communities of faith in which the Christian experience of community, worship, and social concern are integrated in the total experience of students, then parents, and members of the faculty (*Sharing the Light of Faith* 1979, no. 9).

Such a challenge is formidable, to say the least. To meet the challenge successfully, spiritual leadership including faith development must be recognized as central, rather than peripheral, to the very identity of the Catholic school. Human motivations that prompt parents and students to choose Catholic schools are, like all human motivations, complex rather than simple and hybrid rather than homogeneous. Academic excellence, the ability to provide discipline, and the maintenance of a safe learning environment are all easily recognizable qualities that recommend Catholic schools to their constituent publics (Convey 1992). But such characteristics do not embody the *distinct* core purposes of the Catholic school. Vatican II clearly spelled out the mission and purpose of Catholic schools:

- ❧ to create for the school community an atmosphere enlivened by the Gospel spirit of freedom and charity;
- ❧ to help the [student] in such a way that the development of personality will be matched by the growth of the new creation which the [person] became by baptism; and
- ❧ to relate all human culture to the news of salvation, so that the light of faith will illumine the knowledge which students gradually gain of the world, of life, and of [humanity], (*Declaration on Christian Education* 1967, no. 8).

The excellent Catholic school leader is intent on fostering both the religious and academic mission of the Catholic school. First, the principal sees to the spiritual formation of students and faculty "by which one's relationship with the Father becomes more like Jesus': it means being more Christ-like. This is not just a subjective, psychological change, but involves establishing and nurturing a real relationship to Jesus and the Father in the Holy Spirit, through a vigorous sacramental life, prayer, study, and serving others" (*Sharing the Light of Faith* 1979, no. 173). Second, the principal secures the integrity of the academic program by monitoring the teaching and learning process in all subject areas.

Analysis of this twofold mission is enlightened by Sergiovanni (1984) when he explores leadership forces that lead to competence and excellence in schools. Sergiovanni makes a careful distinction between school *competence* and school *excellence*, suggesting that the former is a necessary condition but not an ensurer of the latter. Sergiovanni's conceptualization of these forces can be utilized to enlighten the Catholic school principal's understanding of the responsibility to nurture the faith and spiritual development of students and staff.

According to Sergiovanni, to achieve a competent school, the principal must be able to provide a school environment which is characterized by the following basic forces:

- ❧ **managerial:** the principal utilizes the skills necessary to establish an orderly school environment wherein students and staff can rationally pursue learning;
- ❧ **relational:** the principal successfully builds a human environment of cordiality, respect, and cooperation among students and staff; and

** è&** **educational**: the principal applies the instructional expertise necessary to establish a learning community cognizant of the state-of-the-art knowledge relative to the central school functions of teaching and learning.

But to go beyond competence and to pursue excellence, the principal must possess and apply symbolic and cultural forces. These provide meaning and develop commitment in the lives of the school community:

è& **symbolic**: the principal assumes the role of "chief" by modeling important goals and behaviors and signaling to others a vision of what has meaning and is of importance and value; and

è& **cultural**: the principal articulates the purposes and values of the school, turning doubt into commitment and creating a meaning-filled experience for staff and students.

Although Sergiovanni's remarks (1984) are made about schools in general, much of his vocabulary is very familiar to Catholic school leaders: "School culture includes values, symbols, beliefs, and shared meanings of parents, students, teachers, and others conceived as a group or community. Culture governs what is of worth for this group and how members should think, feel, and behave" (p. 9). Our Catholic faith provides theological, philosophical, and historical principles that enliven the terminology Sergiovanni uses to describe culture. The stated and unstated understandings; the customs and tradition; the habits, norms, and expectations; the common meanings and shared assumptions we hold as Catholics are the heart of the Catholic school culture.

> From the first moment that a student sets foot in a Catholic school, he or she ought to have the impression of entering a new environment, one illumined by the light of faith, and having its own unique characteristics . . . everyone should be aware of the living presence of Jesus . . . [his] inspiration must be translated from the ideal into the real. The Gospel spirit should be evident in a Christian Way of thought and life which permeates all facets of the educational [program] (*The Religious Dimension of Education in a Catholic School* 1988, no. 25).

The Catholic school leader applies the forces of leadership to be able to meet the challenge of fostering spiritual growth and formation. It goes without saying that the Catholic school must possess the rudimentary qualities necessary for competence: to be a good school instructionally, to respect and foster good personal interrelationships, and to provide effective, responsible discipline. However, for the Catholic school to become a truly excellent

---

institution, the Catholic school leader must accept the responsibility of articulating a Christian vision. Furthermore the principal must nurture the development of spiritually self-aware and motivated Christian individuals. ". . . [I]nstruction in religious truths is not just one more subject, but is perceived as *the underlying reality* in which a student's experience of learning and living receive their coherence and their deepest meaning" (Buetow 1988).

Without the conscious recognition of this challenge and directed response to the planning and evaluating strategies which are demanded by that recognition, the Catholic school can satisfy itself with mere competence without ever coming to grips with the ultimate challenge to excellence so central to its very existence and identity.

The cultural and symbolic aspects of the Catholic school are essential to its very reason for being. The distinguishing mission of the Catholic school, as well as its ultimate vision and deepest meaning, are inextricably interwoven with the personhood of Jesus Christ. The call of his life, death, and resurrection is central in the lives of all Christians. It is the most significant responsibility of the Catholic school principal to respond to that call and to serve as catalyst and nurturer of the spiritual growth of all component members of the Catholic school community.

> Prime responsibility for creating this unique Christian school climate rests with the teachers, as individuals and as a community. The religious dimension of the school climate is expressed through the celebration of Christian values in Word and Sacrament, in individual behavior, in friendly, harmonious interpersonal relationships, and in ready availability. Through this daily witness, the students will come to appreciate the uniqueness of the environment to which their youth has been entrusted. If it is not present, then there is little left which can make the school Catholic (*The Religious Dimension of Education in a Catholic School* 1988, no. 26).

This admonition charges the principal to assume three critical tasks relating to the staff. First, the principal begins by serving as a transformational leader to motivate, facilitate, and supervise the growth of staff into effective managers of their classrooms and assigned areas. Second, the principal calls the staff to be thoroughly professional while efficiently and effectively cooperating with colleagues in the furtherance of Catholic school goals. This leads to the development of well-prepared instructional leaders possessing a sound understanding of what constitutes effective pedagogy. Finally, the Catholic school principal accepts the daunting challenge of providing a vision of the Catholic school which involves those same staff members with genuine confrontation with their own spirituality.

In regard to the students, the Catholic school leader has similar responsibilities. Along with the intellectual, emotional, social, and physical growth of Catholic school students, the Catholic school principal recognizes that, to be truly excellent, Catholic schools must foster in students that same critical confrontation with their own spirituality. To foster this development, the school provides formational experiences that will enable students to experience the Jesus who is central to the life of the Catholic school.

Be it known to all who enter here
that Christ is the reason for this school,
the unseen but ever present teacher in its classes,
the model of its faculty,
the inspiration of its students.

Wall mural; St. Mary School; Akron, Ohio.
Original source unknown.

To be meaningfully undertaken, these responsibilities must be integrated within the principal's role rather than added to it. There is no aspect of the Catholic school principal's job description that is irrelevant to this important duty. Curriculum development, the allocation and administration of resources, staffing, the supervision and evaluation of staff, and effective discipline are all functions of the Catholic school principalship which interact with the principal's mandate to attend to the spiritual development of members of the school community (Convey 1992).

The following represent opportunities of particular saliency to spiritual and faith development:

Nurturing opportunities for spiritual growth

The principal of the Catholic school models respect for and commitment to the role of nurturer of opportunities for spiritual development in the process of

- developing and administering a budget that exhibits a consistency with the mission and priorities of the school;
- communicating with staff, students, and parents;

- ❧ motivating all personnel to take responsibility for the religious mission of the school;
- ❧ encouraging constant updating in all instructional areas;
- ❧ articulating organizational and specifically Catholic purposes and strategies;
- ❧ scheduling formational and religious activities for students and staff; and
- ❧ (as applicable) inviting the pastor and clergy to visit in the school and to be present for special school/parent events interacting formally and informally with the school community.

Each of these activities provides the principal with an opportunity to recognize and respond to the call to foster spiritual growth and faith development. Each can also be undertaken without reference to that call, but only to the detriment to the principal's role as spiritual leader.

Ensuring quality Catholic religion instruction

Instruction in religion, as in all subjects in the curriculum, must be provided with attention to the appropriateness of the instructional materials, the soundness of the instructional strategies, and the efficacy of the materials used. To be responsive to the principal's role in nurturing the development of faith, the Catholic school principal must be attentive to the formational consequences that emanate from the school's program of religious instruction. Quality instruction in the Catholic faith entails age-appropriate content, sensitive and open presentation and interaction between teacher and student, and personal response on the part of the learner. The Catholic school principal has the obligation not only to see that religion occupies a prominent place in the curriculum but also that religious instruction is approached with appropriate concern for the above issues. Therefore the principal exhibits concern for the quality of religious instruction when

- ❧ hiring qualified personnel in all subject areas but in particular in the area of religious instruction,
- ❧ providing for appropriate supervision of the content and instruction of religion classes, and
- ❧ (as applicable) inviting the parish clergy to teach religion classes on a weekly or periodic basis.

Providing for the celebration of faith

The faith experience of all involved in the Catholic school community transcends the merely curricular and formally instructional. In addition, the principal seeks to provide ample worship opportunities at which the community can celebrate its ultimate identity and meaning. To be met most effectively, this call requires more than simply finding appropriate places in the school calendar. Attention to the preparation of these sacramental as well as para-liturgical events must ensure that these occasions are characterized by qualities of personalization, reflection, and meaningful participation. When careful attention is accorded these qualities, the celebration of faith will occupy rightfully a central place in the life of the Catholic school. Therefore the principal will

- (in parish and interparochial schools) enlist the cooperation and participation of the parish clergy in planning and providing regular opportunities for liturgies and other sacramental celebrations
- (in secondary schools where there is no regular chaplain) make an effort to ask clergy to celebrate who have the interest and gifts to relate effectively to adolescent students.

Supporting practices of Christian service

As an integral component of the Catholic school mission, the opportunity for members of the school community to provide Christian service demands direct attention and support of the principal. In order to provide a quality response to this responsibility, the Catholic school principal cannot be content to treat this issue simply as a matter of scheduling and material support. Truly educative Christian service opportunities are characterized by

- a degree of selectivity and decision making on the part of participants,
- adult oversight to provide supervisory monitoring and evaluation,
- reflective components, and
- (as applicable) a concern to coordinate with the needs of the parish.

Essential to providing opportunities for Christian service is to allow opportunities for students to commit to the Christian value of leading one's life for others. The injunctions of the Beatitudes and the responsibilities flowing from our baptismal commitment call us to be sensitive to all those around us. Freedom, input, critical evaluation, and reflection are all integral to that purpose.

Reflection Questions

1. Consider and identify opportunities to attend to the principal's responsibilities in the area of faith formation that develop out of each of these important duties:

   - budget development;
   - communicating with staff, parents, students;
   - motivating;
   - articulating organizational purposes and strategies;
   - scheduling.

2. Identify the steps you would take to verify the presence of the following characteristics in the religious instruction program:

   - faithfulness,
   - openness,
   - personal meaning.

3. Identify some practical steps you would take to ensure that your school's liturgical and paraliturgical activities are undertaken with attention to an appropriate degree of personalization and participation for participants.

4. Reflect on the importance of the following qualities in a school's program of Christian service:

   - placement,
   - decision making on the part of participants,
   - evaluation,
   - reflection,
   - (if applicable) concern for the needs of the parish.

Resources

Abbott, W. M., ed. 1966. *Declaration on Christian education (Gravissimum educationis)*. In *The documents of Vatican II*, trans. Joseph Gallagher. New York: The Guild Press.

Bernardin, J. 1989. Catholic schools: Opportunities and challenges. *Chicago Studies*, 28(3):211–16.

Buetow, H. A. 1988. *The Catholic school: Its roots, identity, and future*. New York: Crossroad Publishing Company.

Burns, J. M. 1978. *Leadership*. New York: Harper and Row.

Congregation for Catholic Education. 1988. *The religious dimension of education in a Catholic school*. Washington, D.C.: United States Catholic Conference.

Convey, J. J. 1992. *Catholic schools make a difference*. Washington, D.C.: National Catholic Educational Association.

Covey, S. R. 1991. *Principle-centered leadership*. New York: Simon and Schuster.

De Pree, M. 1992. *Leadership jazz*. New York: Doubleday.

National Conference of Catholic Bishops. 1972. *To teach as Jesus did: A pastoral message on Catholic education*. Washington, D.C.: United States Catholic Conference.

———. 1979. *Sharing the light of faith: National catechetical directory for Catholics of the United States*. Washington, D.C.: United States Catholic Conference.

Pistone, A. J. 1987. Nourishing the faith life of the teacher. *Momentum* 18(1):47.

Ramsey, D. A. 1991. *Empowering leaders*. Kansas City: Sheed and Ward.

Sergiovanni, T. J. 1984. Leadership and excellence in schooling. *Educational Leadership* 41(5):4–13.

The author, Robert Muccigrosso, Ph.D., is the principal of Nazareth Regional High School in Brooklyn, New York.

Christian Community: The Principal's Challenge

Jack Curran, FSC

The enterprise of Catholic education is at the center of the challenge of leadership in the Church today. The Second Vatican Council's understanding of the Church as the "People of God" calls principals to envision the school as a community of faith rather than simply an educational institution (Mann 1991). As a consequence, fundamental to the role of the Catholic school principal is the building up of the People of God, the Church.

"Enduring leadership involves a high degree of personal integrity based on a structured, satisfying, and enriching personal lifestyle" (Ramsey 1991, p. 37). Being aware of one's own spiritual identity and conversant with one's spiritual journey is of utmost importance in the exercise of leadership in the Catholic school. The role of the Catholic school principal encompasses not only the ability to articulate religious values for the community but also the ability to integrate these values into the realities of day-to-day life. Therefore the call to be a spiritual leader demands of the principal a personal spiritual identity that is operative and evident. Ramsey (1991) asserts that the social good contributed to institutions and society by the leader comes from the fundamental quality of the leader's life and work. Research on Catholic school principals (SRI Gallup 1990) indicates principals who make evident their belief in God, witness to their faith, and proclaim publicly the word of God more easily gain the confidence of both parents and teachers. Further, Catholic school principals who have a firm allegiance and strong emotional ties to the Catholic Church as well as a dedication to the profession of education are seen by their teachers to be more genuine in their efforts.

Mattias Neuman (1992) asserts that the key process of all spirituality is integration, being able to sense the presence of God's mysterious activity in the day-to-day details of life. The spiritual leadership of the principal consists of furthering, assisting, and guiding others in this integrative process. The purposeful Catholic school principal is sensitive to others' spiritual needs as well as employment issues, considering each person's faith development as well as occupational responsibilities (Neuman 1992). Such insights and sensitivity not only develop the personal confidence of the principal but also make him or her more credible to teachers, parents, and children.

With growing public scrutiny of all educational institutions, challenges for Catholic school principals continue to accelerate (McGhee 1993). Various constituencies continually demand more time and involvement from the principal. Under the pressures of day-to-day living families and other social institutions often fail to meet and fulfill their responsibilities to children. Frequently these failures place additional stress upon the school and, consequently, upon the principal. The increasing number of demands can be burdensome and somewhat overwhelming at times. However, at other times the exhilaration can be awesome when the principal senses that the children are learning, the teachers are creative, the parents appreciative, and the diocesan officials are satisfied that the school is effective. In order to keep life in its proper perspective the principal strives to maintain rootedness through frequent personal communication with God. The role of principal in a Catholic school is indeed a calling to ministry.

> Be convinced of what St. Paul says, that you plant and water the seed, but it is God through Jesus Christ who makes it grow, that Jesus is the One who brings your work to fulfillment . . . Earnestly ask Jesus Christ to make his Spirit come alive in you, since he has chosen you to do his work (De La Salle ca. 1730/1975).

God has entrusted children to their parents who have in turn entrusted them to the Church and to Catholic schools. God's mysteries are at the heart of the enterprise of Catholic schools: the students, the children of God, are unfolding gifts, wonders of the incarnation, the embodiment of the hope that God promises to the world. Catholic school principals, consequently, endeavor to be attuned to the realities of the movements of God in the lives of the children entrusted to their care in and out of the confines of the school building.

The principal of the Catholic school does not act alone nor in a vacuum and neither do the teachers, students, parents, or diocesan officials. St. Jerome exhorts: "There can be no church community without a leader or team of leaders" (Schillebeeckx 1981). Collaboration in the exercise of leadership is essential for the Catholic school principal not only for successful academic goal attainment but also for overall Christian community building. Principals are called to foster collaboration on a number of levels. Besides with the parents, the Catholic school principal exercises collaborative skills with the parish community as well as with the wider Catholic and non-Catholic community.

In 1988 on the feast day of Saint John Baptist De La Salle, patron of teachers, the Vatican issued a document to promote the renewal of Catholic education: *The Religious Dimension of Education in a Catholic School.* Among the various issues of this document is an invitation for Catholic schools to enter into a self-examination with a goal toward strengthening collaboration and partnership among those involved in the educational process. Schools are cautioned against alienation from families and isolation from the local Church (Mann 1991).

Three specific expectations follow from an understanding of the responsibility of the Catholic school principal to exercise spiritual leadership in the building of Christian community.

Fostering collaboration
between the parish(es) and the school

Thomas (1989) asserts that the responsibilities of the school community transpire within the context of the ministry of the parish. The spiritual development of the children is primarily the responsibility of the parents who turn to the Church for guidance and support. The children in our schools are there because the parents and the Church have entrusted them to the teachers for the purpose of assisting the parents in their God-given work (Mann 1991). The Catholic school and its teachers supplement the work of parents and pastors. Writing in the 17th century, St. John Baptist De La Salle calls us to reflect on the dignity of our ministry in schools, a ministry which is a unique expression of the Church's purpose.

> You must, then, look upon this work entrusted to you by pastors, by fathers and mothers, as one of the most important and most necessary services in the Church (De La Salle ca. 1730/1975).

Mann (1991) emphasizes the call of the Congregation for Catholic Education for mutual esteem and reciprocal collaboration between the Catholic school and church authorities. The person of the principal is the key linchpin in this collaborative dynamic of parent, pastor, teacher (Thomas and Davis 1989). It is incumbent upon the principal in the Catholic school to further communication and collaborative activities among these constituencies in the building up of the People of God who are the Church. In response to this mandate, proactive Catholic school principals frequently invite diocesan officials, superintendents, pastors, and other parish ministers to participate in school events. Since the principal is in a prime position to encourage this spirit of collaboration, Thomas and Davis (1989) recommend that the principal seek to serve as a member of the parish pastoral team. The principal is challenged to nurture a sense of unity with various church and parish organizations. This is of particular concern for Catholic schools whose student body comes from more than one parish. Not only is it incumbent for those in church leadership to work together, but also this leadership ought to provide opportunities for the people who are the Church to "rub elbows." Parents and the staff of the school, parish religion programs, and other parish and diocesan organizations need to come together to know one another and to work together on common projects. As all members of the Christian community collectively take responsibility for fulfilling various roles and functions, coordinating activities, and relying upon each other, the vision of Christian community moves from the "property" of the leadership to being "owned" by all involved. Organizing periodic parish-school or diocesan-school service projects is one way to promote this communal climate. In this manner, then, the vision of Christian community is more likely to be realized (Conger and Kanungo, et al. 1988).

Fostering a collaborative relationship between the Catholic secondary school and feeder parishes is an important responsibility of the high school principal. Regular personal and professional communication with elementary principals concerning curricular programs and extracurricular activities can build a support network that will benefit faculties and students at both levels. Inviting both faculties and students of the feeder parish school to high school events promotes interest and feelings of loyalty to the school. Publicizing the achievements of high school students who are parish elementary school alumni in the parish bulletin can be a cause for celebration for both schools. Encouraging the secondary student's involvement in home parish activities promotes lifelong habits of active parish participation. Recognizing student volunteer participation in the liturgical, religious education, and athletic programs of the parish nurtures leadership talent and self-esteem.

Recognizing, respecting, and facilitating the role of parents as primary educators

The Vatican II Council's *Declaration on Christian Education* (1966) is particularly significant in stating that Catholic schools "are invited to assist parents" (no. 5). It is as partners with parents that Catholic schools perform their work for the Church.

Support for parent-teacher collaboration is also found in the *Code of Canon Law*:

It is incumbent upon parents to cooperate closely with the school teachers to whom they entrust their children to be educated; in fulfilling their duties teachers are to collaborate closely with parents who are to be willingly heard and for whom associations or meetings are to be inaugurated and held in great esteem (no. 796).

Since nothing less than the very future of the world and of the Church is affected by the quality of Catholic schools today, Pope John Paul II states that new forms of cooperation between parents and teachers are needed. In *On the Family* (1982) he makes an urgent appeal for pastoral efforts to support and strengthen families at this present moment in history (Mann 1991). As the leader, the Catholic school principal is commissioned to align the resources of the school and the parish church community toward enhancing the work of the primary educators of children, the parents. In support of this partnership, the Vatican Congregation for Catholic Education in *The Religious Dimension of Education in a Catholic School* (1988) states that "it is impossible to do too much along these lines" (no. 43).

Elinor Ford (1992) issues a strong call regarding families, Catholic schools, and faith. In order for teaching to take place, Ford maintains, the three constituents of youngster, teacher, and family need to be involved actively. It takes "three to teach." Ford focuses especially on the dynamic process of awakening faith and the role of the Home-School Association. The Catholic school principal demonstrates Christian community leadership in promoting home-school faith-sharing activities. Among the various opportunities involving the family and the school in faith sharing are retreats and liturgical experiences. In consultation with school and parish personnel the Home-School Association is an excellent vehicle to sponsor these activities.

Teachers, researchers, and administrators attest to the positive impact of parental involvement in school activities upon student achievement (Bennett and LeCompte 1990, Coleman 1987, Epstein 1987). The Catholic school principal demonstrates effective leadership when enlisting the involvement of parents in the life of the school. Opportunities for volunteering in the school, for serving on various committees and boards, and for presenting lessons in classrooms are some examples of ways parents might be meaningfully involved in their children's education. The creative principal will elicit parental involvement and make it an integral and vital aspect of the school experience.

Secondary school principals can be helpful particularly to parents of adolescent students. Communicating with parents about the expectations of the school and working with parents to set reasonable limits for their children are two ways the school can sustain parents as they cope with the trials and tribulations of adolescent development. Facilitating networks of parents in similar home situations (single, widowed, native language, neighborhoods) will provide additional parenting support. Encouraging "newcomer" parents to be involved in school activities and introducing them to the "veteran" parents at the school will promote community at that level and provide opportunities for parents to share and reinforce their common values.

Promoting Catholic community

Vatican Council II highlighted the essential role of community in the life of the Church. The Council reconceptualized the image of the Catholic school from being an institution into the realization that it is essentially a community of people. Recent church teachings on education emphasize the necessity of the professionals in schools to collaborate with parents and pastors in the forming of a truly Christian community (cf. *Declaration on Christian Education* 1966, *On the Family* 1982, *The Religious Dimension of Education in a Catholic School* 1988). Awareness of our unity as the People of God both motivates and compels the principal to encourage the formation of Christian community.

Community is a concept that must be lived and can best be learned by experiencing it (*To Teach as Jesus Did* no. 23). The composite ways that people live, work, pray, and play constitute what is meant by community (Neuman 1987). Interdependence, the dignity of each person, hospitality, and reconciliation are hallmarks of Catholic community. Developing curricula that welcome and support diverse cultural and economic populations is in service of the building of Christian community. Rejecting racism, sexism, and other forms of discrimination in what is said as well as in what is done is the duty of the Catholic school principal. School activities enhancing cultural awareness, ecumenism, and reconciliation are activities that the principal must promote. These activities form the web that binds and builds the People of God.

Having the energy and altruism of adolescents as a resource, the Catholic secondary principal is in a natural position to promote the Catholic community. Religious education programs often build service hours and courses into the curriculum. Students can be encouraged to offer their time and talents to Catholic and civic organizations that embody Christian values. For instance, high school students can be powerful role models for younger children and ambassadors of concern to the elderly and homebound. Involvement in such activities not only promotes community but also provides invaluable experience and widens the horizons of the young person by enfleshing the Beatitudes and enlivening gospel values.

The fiery vision that unites people, the quality of their bondedness is the essence of community according to Woodward (1987). Solidarity, mutual commitment, the sharing of hopes and values are among the goals of the collaborative interactions aimed at building community. These intangible but essential realities are at the heart of the Catholic school principal's role in promoting Catholic community.

Reflection Questions

1. As a Catholic school principal what is your reaction to the words of Saint John Baptist De La Salle?

    > Since you are ambassadors and ministers of Jesus Christ in the work that you do, you must act as representing Jesus Christ himself. . . . In order to fulfill your responsibility with as much perfection and care as God requires of you, frequently give yourself to the Spirit of our Lord to act only under his influence. . . . (De La Salle, ca 1730/1975).

    Give examples of ways you will live these maxims in your daily work.

2. Thomas (1989) places the functioning of the school within the context of the parish. He suggests that the principal be a part of the pastoral team of the parish.

     What is your experience of this intimate connection of the school and parish?

- ❧ What could you do to encourage a spirit of collaboration? OR as a high school principal, how will you develop and engender a team spirit among your administrative staff?

- ❧ How do you motivate *every* teacher (coach, librarian, etc.) in the school, regardless of the subjects taught, to take personal responsibility for building Christian community within his or her classroom?

- ❧ What pastoral considerations will you bring to your efforts?

3. The church documents since Vatican II speak of the school as assisting the primary educators of children, the parents of the children. Considering the realities of your school community situation, how will you enhance your school's assistance of parents in the education of their children?

4. Woodward (1987) asserts that community is defined by the fiery vision that unites people.

- ❧ What is the vision around which you sense that members of your school and parish community are united?

- ❧ What leadership behaviors might you and your school staff undertake to foster unity among the generational groups in the parish and civic community?

The author, Jack Curran, FSC, is a doctoral student at the State University of New York in Rochester, New York.

Resources

Abbott, W. M., ed. 1966. *Declaration on Christian education (Gravissimum educationis)*. In *The documents of Vatican II*, trans. Joseph Gallagher. New York: The Guild Press.

Bennett, K. P., and M. D. LeCompte. 1990. *How schools work: A sociological analysis of education*. White Plains, N.Y.: Longman.

Coleman, J. 1987. *Public and private high schools: The impact of communities*. New York: Basic Books.

Conger, J. A., R. N. Kanungo, et al. 1988. *Charismatic leadership, the elusive factor in organizational effectiveness*. San Francisco: Jossey-Bass Publishers.

Congregation for Catholic Education. 1988. *The religious dimension of education in a Catholic school: Guidelines for reflection and renewal*. Washington, D.C.: United States Catholic Conference.

De La Salle, J. B. [ca. 1730] 1975. *Meditations for the time of retreat*. Trans. A. Loes. Romeoville, Ill.: Christian Brothers Conference.

Epstein, J. L. 1987. Toward a theory of family-school connections: Teachers' practices and parent involvement across school years. In *Social intervention: Potential and constraints*, ed. D. Hurrelmann, F. Kaufmann, and F. Losel. New York: de Grutra Press.

Ford, E. R. 1992. Faith alive: A wake-up call. *Today's Catholic Teacher* 25(7):50–54.

John Paul II. 1982. *On the family (Familiaris consortio)*. Washington, D.C.: United States Catholic Conference.

Kealey, R. 1989. The unique dimension of the Catholic school. *Momentum* 20(1):29.

Mann, W. E. 1991. *The Lasallian school: Where teachers assist parents in the education and formation of children*. Narragansett, R.I.: Brothers of the Christian Schools, Long Island-New England Province, Inc.

McGhee, C. 1993. Barefoot prophets. *Momentum* 24(3):55.

National Conference of Catholic Bishops. 1972. *To teach as Jesus did: A pastoral message on Catholic education*. Washington, D.C.: United States Catholic Conference.

———. 1979. *Sharing the light of faith: National catechetical directory for Catholics of the United States*. Washington, D.C.: United States Catholic Conference.

Neuman, M. 1987. Modern media and the religious sense of community. *Review for Religious* 46(2):195–201.

———. 1992. Pastoral leadership beyond the managerial. *Review for Religious* 51(4):585–94.

Ramsey, D. A. 1991. *Empowering leaders*. Kansas City: Sheed and Ward.

Schillebeeckx, E. 1981. *Ministry, leadership in the community of Jesus Christ*. New York: Crossroad Publishing Company.

SRI Gallup. 1990. Themes of the Catholic school principal. In *The Catholic school principal perceiver: Concurrent validity report*. Lincoln, Neb.: Human Resources for Ministry Institute.

Thomas, J. A., and B. Davis. 1989. The principal as part of the pastoral team. In *Reflections on the role of the Catholic school principal*, ed. R. Kealey. Washington, D.C.: National Catholic Educational Association.

Woodward, E. 1987. *Poets, prophets and pragmatists: A new challenge to religious life*. Notre Dame, Ind.: Ave Maria Press.

Moral and Ethical Development: The Principal's Charge

Robert Muccigrosso, Ph.D.

There is no denying that American society, as it approaches the millennium, is characterized by a lack of moral consensus. People of all ages attest to this concern whether one remembers the day of President John F. Kennedy's assassination in 1963, the morally confusing and politically disastrous role of the United States in Vietnam in the late '60s, the public shame of a president forced from office in the aftermath of the Watergate scandal, the insider trading in the stock market, or some less dramatic and obvious moment or movement.

Evidence of the moral battle raging and threatening to tear apart our society can be found in the abortion controversy, in the diametrically opposed educational responses to the AIDS crisis, as well as on the front pages of our newspapers. The media is astute at keeping us apprised of the latest moral failure in the worlds of politics, finance, and business.

The very essence of public education demands that it reflect the larger society that sponsors and finances it. But in the pluralistic society of the United States where there is no broad-based agreement on values, the public school is often caught in the dilemma as it carries out its mission. Prayer in the schools, discipline, sex education, and curriculum are just a few of the areas of public school life which reflect the ambiguities inherent in today's moral climate.

The Catholic school, while certainly not immune to differences of opinion concerning moral issues, freely embraces without ambiguity its responsibility for the moral education of its students. It draws great strength from moral and ethical principles which are cornerstones of the Christian value system in general and of the Catholic faith in particular.

> The Catholic school finds its true justification in the mission of the Church; it is based on an educational philosophy in which faith, culture, and life are brought into harmony. Through it, the local Church evangelizes, educates, and contributes to the healthy and morally sound life-style among its members (*The Religious Dimension of Education in a Catholic School* 1988, no. 34).

While there may well be differences of opinion regarding how education in sexuality, for instance, might most effectively be undertaken, there is clear recognition of the fact that the value system at the foundation of the Catholic school will be based on the values of chastity, respect for the sanctity of the human body, respect for the responsibilities of those in different states of life, and promotion of the values of marriage and family.

In today's moral climate, then, there is a sense in which the Catholic school must accept a degree of counter-culturalism as part of its identity.

> It is one of the formal tasks of a [Catholic] school, as an institution for education, to draw out the ethical dimension for the precise purpose of arousing the individual's inner spiritual dynamism and to aid his achieving that moral freedom which complements the psychological. Behind this moral freedom, however, stand those absolute values which alone give meaning and value to human life. This has to be said because the tendency to adopt present-day values as a yardstick is not absent even in the educational world. The danger is always to react to passing, superficial ideas and to lose sight of the much deeper needs of the contemporary world (*The Catholic School* 1977, no. 30).

Most powerfully—beyond the Catholic school's stated moral posture, beyond the Catholic school's explicitly value-oriented curriculum—the moral and ethical example of the Catholic school establishes its moral credibility and its own value as a visible sign of the Christian message in contact with, and hopefully transforming, the world. If the Catholic school is to play a significant role in the building of the City of God, that role must begin with the example of its own moral clarity and Gospel orientation. The Catholic school, as other human endeavors, will on occasion fall short of its own moral ideals. However, the Catholic school which forgets or subordinates those ideals does so at the risk of denying its own principles.

Since there is just one truth, it is not surprising but particularly instructive to look at research in the area of leadership. Conducted in the very secular environment of corporate America, the results repeatedly find that moral integrity is high among the personal qualities most frequently perceived to be characteristic of effective leaders (Covey 1989, 1991; De Pree 1989; Ramsey 1991). Moral leadership is a powerful expectation of followers in any aspect of the leadership role—political, psychological, organizational. Integrity in dealing with others is rated high by those evaluating effectiveness of leaders (De Pree 1989). "From moral leadership 'comes' purposing, building a covenant of shared values, one that binds people in a common cause and transforms a school from an organization to a community" (Sergiovanni 1992, p. 15).

The keeper of the Catholic school's moral gate is the principal. Central to this gate-keeping function is the principal's responsibility to keep the Catholic moral vision constantly before all who comprise the Catholic school community. "The leader is responsible for the set of ethics or norms that governs the behavior of people in the organization" (Bennis and Nanus 1988, p. 186).

The principal of the Catholic school is at the nexus of these influences—curricular, co-curricular, formational, interpersonal—which comprise the moral education promoted by the Catholic school. The specifics of this charge work their way through the hours and minutes of the school calendar in dozens of individual ways. An effective program of moral and ethical development must include outreach to the cognitive (knowing), the affective (feeling), and the active (service-oriented) areas of life (Elias 1989).

Just a few of the obvious ways in which the principal of the Catholic school establishes the school's moral message and ethical climate are through the hiring and evaluating the staff, reflecting the school's priorities through budget decisions, defining the curriculum, administering discipline, and articulating the school's moral vision in countless informal ways to students, staff, and parents.

Several particularly salient principles emerge and are central to the issue of the institutional integrity of the Catholic school.

Inclusivity

The moral vision of the Catholic school must stand for an inclusive relationship with its constituencies. Some threats to this quality are obvious. Purposeful racial homogeneity is obviously a value inconsistent with the Christian ethic and Catholic social policy. Other forms of exclusivity, however, are less obvious and, therefore, perhaps more dangerous. Distinctions based on economic class and academic ability can easily insinuate themselves into Catholic schools.

While meeting their fiscal responsibilities, Catholic school principals need to be vigilant in managing their resources in order to keep their schools financially accessible to as many students as possible. Leadership needs to be exerted to support programs and financial policies which will allow and encourage those with more means to help those in the school community with fewer means. Grant programs, "adopt-a-student" programs of tuition assistance, and the funding of scholarship programs are all initiatives worthy of Catholic school leadership.

Another subtle form of exclusivity can be found in distinctions based on academic or intellectual ability levels. Catholic schools are called to be responsive to the learning needs of children and young adults at all places on the learning continuum. Indeed, even inside the individual Catholic school, principals do well to examine all distinctions related to membership in the school community—gender or ability-driven—to ensure that they are founded solidly in programmatic reality rather than in blind adherence to institutional tradition or preferences.

Another facet of inclusivity merits discussion here, that is the trend of Catholic schools to enroll students of other religious persuasions. Guidance in this area comes from the direct exhortation of the Congregation for Catholic Education:

> Not all students are members of the Catholic Church; not all are Christians. . . . The religious freedom and personal conscience of individual students and their families must be respected. . . . On the other hand, a Catholic school cannot relinquish its own freedom to proclaim the Gospel and to offer a formation based on the values to be found in a Christian education; this is its right and duty. To proclaim or to offer is not to impose, however; the latter suggests a moral violence which is strictly forbidden, both by the Gospel and by Church law (*The Religious Dimension of Education in a Catholic School* 1988, no. 6).

Supportiveness

The Catholic school, founded on the life and teachings of Jesus Christ, must serve as a sign of Jesus' message of the worth and sacredness of the individual. Without sacrificing intellectual vigor or formational expectations for the personal growth of all involved, the Catholic school must strive to embody the Christian concern for the "least among My brethren." It matters not whether that "least" is defined in terms of intellectual giftedness, developmental delays in the areas of social or physical growth, or difficulty assuming responsibility for personal self-discipline; all deserve to be treated with dignity. It might be foolish and, perhaps, counterproductive, for each individual Catholic school to assert its ability to succeed with every youngster. However, the decision to exclude those who experience problems in responding to the school's academic, social, or formational programs should be reached only after it is clear that the school has done all within its power to succeed with that youngster while simultaneously being responsive to the needs of the other members of the school community. Moreover, the Catholic school, under the leadership of the principal, needs to be vigilant in articulating, establishing, and maintaining a school climate that is assertive in insisting on the value of all those who comprise the school community who are the "children of God." Therefore, the principal has a specific responsibility to model attitudes and to impress upon all staff members the critical need to hold reasonable yet high expectations of all students regardless of the possible educational limitations in the student's personal background. Such behavior underlines the worth of every person who "has an inalienable right to an education . . . suited to . . . native talent, sex, cultural background and ancestral heritage" (*Declaration on Christian Education* 1966, no. 1).

Clarity

Catholic teaching recounting the relationship between church teaching on moral and ethical questions and the demands of the honestly and vigorously developed individual conscience acknowledges that respect is due to both sources of moral decision making and behavior. Working as a staff member at a Catholic school does not involve sacrificing one's God-given competence and duty to develop an informed conscience. At the same time, those working in Catholic schools need to exert care to see that all speak with one voice when formally involved in the educational and evangelizing activities of the school. That voice must be consistent with the Catholic identity of the school. Intellectual vigor and honesty demand age-appropriate exploration of the various perspectives of a moral or ethical question. But in such instances, the responsibility of the Catholic school staff is to be sure the official position of the Catholic Church is made clear and understood by the students. The destructiveness of speech or behavior on the part of individual staff members which is at odds with the orthodox teaching of the Church too often can have serious and painful consequences, especially for impressionable youth. The Catholic school principal needs to exert leadership in the school in pursuit of a clear teaching voice for the Catholic school as representative of the institutional Church:

... [I]t is necessary to do everything possible to see to it that judgments of conscience are informed and in accord with the moral order of God which is creator. Common sense requires that conscientious people be open and humble, ready to learn from the experience and insights of others, willing to acknowledge prejudices and even change their judgments in light of better instruction. Above and beyond this, followers of Jesus will have a realistic approach to conscience which leads them to accept what He taught and judge things as He judges them (*Sharing the Light of Faith* 1979, no. 103).

Two specific competencies develop from a concern for the moral and ethical integrity of the school and the development of youth.

To Facilitate the Moral Development and Maturity of Children, Youth, and Adults

The Catholic school principal labors assiduously to establish the Catholic school as an entity in which moral and ethical questions reside at the center of the school's identity.

The Catholic school effort can be distinguished from its public and nonsectarian private counterparts by its willingness to accept responsibility for the development of the entire personhood of all who comprise the school community. Rather than shirking the moral and ethical implications of knowledge and formation, the Catholic school asserts the primacy of moral and ethical behavior as the fulfillment of all its teaching and formational outreaches.

Catholic school principals undertake the responsibility to foster an atmosphere in which this centrality is professed with enthusiasm and confidence. "The integration of religious truth and values with the rest of life is brought about in the Catholic school not only by its unique curriculum, but also by the presence of teachers who express an integrated approach to learning and living in their private and professional lives" (*To Teach as Jesus Did* 1972, no. 103).

With particular emphasis on preserving the rightful place in the curriculum for frequent reminders of the moral and ethical implications of learning in the various fields of knowledge, the principal strives to create a learning atmosphere that never allows these implications to be forgotten or subordinated.

By vigilantly promoting opportunities for Christian service, the Catholic school principal strengthens the primacy of moral and ethical behavior as the fullest realization of the gospel message and example:

You address me as "Teacher" and "Lord" and fittingly enough, for that is what I am. But if I washed your feet—I who am Teacher and Lord—then you must wash each other's feet. What I just did was to give you an example: as I have done, so you must do (Jn 13:13–15).

To Integrate Gospel Values and Christian Ethics into the Curriculum Policies and Life of the School

The Catholic school principal as the educational leader of the school is essentially a "teacher" among teachers. "Find a school with a healthy moral environment and . . . you'll find a principal who is leading the way" (Lickona 1991, p. 325). Through speech and particularly through behavior, the principal communicates a moral vision.

In establishing and administering policies and procedures concerning school discipline, the principal most obviously evidences a particular approach to moral and ethical development. This approach is founded on knowledge of how children grow in the moral and ethical domain and characterized by a devotion to values of justice and peacemaking (cf. Traviss 1985).

As employer, the Catholic school principal speaks and behaves with great moral and ethical weight and responsibility. Selecting, supervising, evaluating, and compensating staff are all activities whereby the principal can display an understanding of and an adherence to the principles of justice and peacemaking.

Resolving conflicts between students, between students and adults, and between adults is another demand placed on the principal which is laden with implications for the moral and ethical development of all involved. In interacting with parents, the principal is called to demonstrate an appropriate respect for the parents' role as the primary educators of their children. Further, the principal will want to foster a degree of collaboration between school and parent that can contribute greatly and productively to the growth of the student, staff, parent, and local community.

In situations where schools are associated with one or more parishes, principals will want to enlist the talent and expertise of the pastor, parish staff, and school board members in rendering leadership relating to moral and ethical matters.

Reflection Questions

1. Do your school's admission and retention policies evidence the Christian values of inclusivity, patience, and openness? How are they inconsistent with this challenge?

2. As employer, does your school behave in a manner consistent with the dignity of the worker in general and with church social policy in particular? Specify potential problems in this area.

3. As you review your school's disciplinary policies, are you satisfied that they reflect an appropriate emphasis on individual growth in self-discipline? What improvements can be made in this area?

4. Review the various components of the job description of the principal in your school. How many opportunities to articulate and model Christian leadership in the area of moral development can you identify?

5. Does the school foster opportunities for students to perform Christian service? How is this accomplished? How is this service experience evaluated?

6. Does your school's curriculum provide students with meaningful opportunities to examine contemporary moral issues of war and peace, materialism, consumerism, sexuality, and family? How is the Church's teaching in these areas reflected in these contexts?

Resources

Abbott, W. M., ed. 1966. *Declaration on Christian education (Gravissimum educationis)*. In *The documents of Vatican II*, trans. Joseph Gallagher. New York: The Guild Press.

Bennis, W. A., and B. Nanus. 1988. *Leaders*. New York: Harper and Row.

Congregation for Catholic Education. 1977. *The Catholic school*. Washington, D.C.: United States Catholic Conference.

———. 1988. *The religious dimension of education in a Catholic school: Guidelines for reflection and renewal*. Washington, D.C.: United States Catholic Conference.

Covey, S. R. 1989. *The seven habits of highly effective people*. New York: Simon and Schuster.

———. 1991. *Principle-centered leadership*. New York: Simon and Schuster.

De Pree, M. 1989. *Leadership is an art*. New York: Doubleday.

Elias, J. 1989. *Moral education: Secular and religious*. Malabar, Fla.: R. E. Krieger Publishers.

Lickona, T. 1991. *Educating for character*. New York: Bantam Books.

National Conference of Catholic Bishops. 1972. *To teach as Jesus did: A pastoral message on Catholic education*. Washington, D.C.: United States Catholic Conference.

———. 1979. *Sharing the light of faith: National catechetical directory for Catholics of the United States*. Washington, D.C.: United States Catholic Conference.

Nucci, L., ed. 1989. *Moral development and character education*. Berkeley, Calif.: McCutchan Publisher.

Ramsey, D. A. 1991. *Empowering leaders*. Kansas City: Sheed and Ward.

Sergiovanni, T. J. 1992. *Moral leadership: Getting to the heart of school improvement*. San Francisco: Jossey-Bass Publishers.

Sergiovanni, T. J., and J. E. Corbally. 1986. *Leadership and organizational culture*. Chicago: University of Illinois Press.

Traviss, M. P. 1985. *Student moral development in the Catholic school*. Washington, D.C.: National Catholic Educational Association.

The author, Robert Muccigrosso, Ph.D., is the principal of Nazareth Regional High School in Brooklyn, New York.

History and Philosophy: The Principal's Foundation

Robert J. Kealey, Ed.D.

To fully understand American Catholic school education in the closing days of the twentieth century, a person needs an appreciation of its history and a grasp of the philosophy upon which this system of over 8,000 schools educating nearly three million students is built. In this short paper the entire story of Catholic schools cannot be told nor can the voluminous literature related to the philosophy of Catholic schools be reviewed. Therefore, twelve events in the history of Catholic schools will be briefly cited and a brief reflection given on how each of these events demonstrates that the philosophy of Catholic schools is a lived reality. The reader will discover that philosophy and history are intimately connected. Some historical events flowed from the philosophical foundation for Catholic schools and other events helped shape the philosophy of Catholic schools.

1606: An integrated education

In this year the Franciscan friars opened a school in St. Augustine, Fla. This was one of the earliest Catholic schools in what was to become the United States. The founding documents of this school proclaimed its purpose, "to teach children Christian doctrine, reading and writing." This school continued to provide this integrated education until 1753. The Catholic philosophy of education dictated that Catholic schools had a twofold mission: to assist in the evangelization of the students and to provide youth with a fundamental education. Philadelphia's first Catholic school opened 175 years later and echoed this dual purpose. The founding documents stated that St. Mary School was to be a place "where the young might be instructed in their religion and receive secular education as well."

This same integration of learning can be found in the mission statements of most Catholic schools founded since these two schools. Catholic educators recognize the totality of the human person. A person's life is not divided into parts, but one's religious values impact all aspects of life. This approach to education is unique to Catholic schools and other religious schools. Christian values are examined in all curriculum areas and are reflected in all aspects of the school. The 1988 document from the Vatican Congregation for Catholic Education, *The Religious Dimension of Education in a Catholic School,* clearly stated this point, "The Catholic school finds its true justification in the mission of the Church; it is based on an educational philosophy in which faith, culture and life are brought into harmony" (no. 34).

1727: An education for all of society

Ursuline Academy opened in 1727 in New Orleans and continues to educate more than 700 children today; it has the distinction of being the oldest continuously operating Catholic school in the United States. This school had three divisions when it first opened: a boarding school for the daughters of the aristocrats of New Orleans; a day school for the children of the merchant class; and religion classes taught by the sisters for the African American and Native American children.

This school demonstrates that American Catholic schools always sought to address the needs of all social and economic groups in society. Later in the history of Catholic schools, several religious communities of women would be founded specifically to educate some of the poorest and most deprived in American society.

In creating Ursuline Academy with these various divisions, the sisters established a practice that would be followed by many other religious communities in the United States. The sisters conducted a school for the wealthy and charged a tuition. This provided the religious community with the needed funds for its existence and allowed other sisters to teach the children of the working class and poor without having to charge them tuition. Thus from the very beginning of Catholic education in the United States a procedure was established to finance the education of all children no matter what their socioeconomic level. Catholic school educators take up the command of Jesus to "teach all nations" (Mt 28:19).

1802: Role of the laity in evangelization

In February of this year, St. Peter School on Barclay Street in New York City opened with a faculty of four: Fr. O'Brien and Messrs. Morris, Neylan, and Heing. Eleven months before the opening of the school, a group of parents approached the pastor and requested him to open a school for their children. The pastor referred the matter to the lay board of trustees that governed the parish. After almost a year's discussion the school opened. In this early period of Catholic education, many schools came into existence because parents in the local area wanted a Catholic school for their children and the board, which represented these parishioners, recognized that the parish would be able to meet its financial commitment to maintain the school. St. Peter School opened with a predominately lay faculty which reflected the multicultural community of early New York City.

While priests and especially pastors are richly deserving of the credit that is given to them in being instrumental in founding Catholic schools, they could not have done this without the support of the laity. The pennies, nickels, and dimes they contributed each Sunday in the offertory collections built the present-day system of Catholic schools. While today may be called the age of the laity, the People of God in the United States always assisted in the evangelization of the next generation of Catholics. The school always served an important function in the Catholic Church's mission of evangelization. The Vatican Congregation for Catholic Education wrote, "[The Catholic school] is a place of evangelization, of authentic apostolate and of pastoral action—not through complementary or parallel or extracurricular activity, but of its very nature; its work of educating the Christian person" (*The Religious Dimension of Education in a Catholic School* 1988, no. 33). The laity have always been involved in it.

1808: Commitment to excellence

St. Elizabeth Ann Seton founded the Sisters of Charity in 1808 and undertook the task of educating sisters to provide a total religious education in Catholic schools. Her formal procedures for the training of future teachers represented the first school of teacher preparation in the United States. Throughout the rest of the nineteenth century numerous religious communities were established in the United States with the express mission of teaching in Catholic schools. In addition many European communities of sisters followed the immigrants to these shores and continued to minister to them in American Catholic schools. While lay teachers continued to play an important role in Catholic schools, the number of sisters grew so that by the middle of this century over 85 percent of the teachers in Catholic schools were women religious.

The personal sacrifices of these thousands of women religious made Catholic schools what they are today. Their personal and professional integration of the principles of the Gospel with the world of knowledge gave

Catholic schools their unique character. The sisters also endowed Catholic schools with two other characteristics. The sisters were excellent teachers. With practically nothing they transformed cold barren classrooms into true centers of learning. They devised numerous teaching strategies to meet the needs of children with all kinds of learning problems. Second, the sisters believed in children. They instilled in students a desire to learn and the confidence that they could learn. Today, the American Catholic community is the best educated in the entire family of the United States. This commitment to excellence is the legacy of the religious communities of women.

1884: Supportive environment

The American bishops met in Baltimore in 1884 in their Third Council and decreed that near every church a Catholic school was to be built within two years. The motivation for this decree was the lack of willingness on the part of the government schools to allow the reading of the Catholic Bible and the teaching of the Catholic religion in the schools. Given the present state of the education offered in government-owned and -operated schools, one may find it hard to believe that at one time the reading of the Bible, the saying of prayers, and the teaching of religion were common practices in such schools. However, Catholics did not approve of the Bible readings or the lessons given in the mid-nineteenth century; they were decidedly Protestant and even anti-Catholic. Some of the stories in the early editions of the famous McGuffey readers manifested the anti-Catholic feeling found in government-controlled schools.

While the creation of Catholic schools may seem like a defense mechanism, their establishment really illustrated how people exercised their power to demand that schools satisfy their needs. People have viewed this move as Catholics turning in on themselves. While some truth may be found in this proposition, the effects of this inward turning are just the opposite. Catholics received from their schools a deeper concern about the larger community especially in terms of social justice issues than any other group in American society. The goal of situating a school near every church was never achieved. In 1965, when more Catholic students were in Catholic schools than ever before, only 59 percent of the parishes had Catholic schools. The bishops' pronouncement of 1884 highlights the supportive environment that Catholic schools provide in the evangelization of youth. That is why, in 1990, the American Catholic bishops set for themselves the goal, "That serious efforts

---

will be made to ensure that Catholic schools are available for Catholic parents who wish to send their children to them" (*In Support of Catholic Elementary and Secondary Schools* 1990, p. 6).

1890: Continuing the education process

In 1890 the Archdiocese of Philadelphia opened Roman Catholic High School which was the first central (diocesan) high school; it continues to operate to this day. While many religious communities had established academies, these by and large were attended by more affluent students because the general population entered the work force after completing a few years of school. Therefore, this event in Philadelphia signified that Catholic education was now moving to higher levels for all students and was no longer just concerned with primary education. The event also indicated that the support for Catholic schools was no longer limited to parents or the local parish, but now the whole diocese was called upon to contribute to the support of the school. At the present time, about 35 percent of the Catholic secondary schools are diocesan, about 25 percent parish or interparochial, and about 41 percent private. Today, through their various programs, Catholic schools involve more adults in formal programs of ongoing spiritual formation and education than any other agency of the Catholic Church.

1904: Professional educators

In this year Catholic education truly came of age and acknowledged that those involved in it were both ministers of the Catholic Church and professional educators. In St. Louis that summer, under the leadership of the Rev. Francis Howard, superintendent of schools for the Diocese of Columbus, three existing Catholic educational associations agreed to form one association with three departments. The original associations were the Educational Conference of Seminary Faculties (1898), the Association of Catholic Colleges (1899), and the Parish School Conference (1902). The new Catholic Educational Association, in the view of the co-founders, was to be a symbol of unity and provide professional help to its members. The three issues that the association devoted its time to in the early years attested to these goals: the length and nature of the elementary school curriculum, the standardization of Catholic colleges, and the role of the nation's hierarchy in fostering Catholic educational unity. The rapid growth of the association was acknowledged in 1927 when the word "national" was added to its title. The present NCEA constitution in its first article states, "The National Catholic Educational Association, the professional association for all Catholic educators, advances the total educational mission of the church. . . ."

1925: First educators

A few years prior to this date, the state of Oregon passed a law which required all children to be educated in state controlled schools. The Sisters of the Holy Names of Jesus and Mary at St. Mary School in Portland sued the state over this law. In this year the case, *Pierce v. the Society of Sisters*, was heard by the U.S. Supreme Court. The court declared, "The fundamental theory of liberty upon which all governments in this Union repose excludes any general power of the State to standardize its children by forcing them to accept instruction from public teachers only. The child is not the mere creature of the State; those who nurture him and direct his destiny have the right, coupled with the high duty, to recognize and prepare him for additional obligations" (268 U.S. 510).

Thus the U.S. Supreme Court established as constitutional law the fact that parents have the first responsibility to educate their children, a truth that Catholic school educators have always held. The Catholic school exists to assist the parents with the education of their children. This constitutional case established the principle that parents have the right to choose the school they believe is best for their children; this created the foundation for the present discussion of parental choice in education.

1947: Equality

America at this time was just emerging from World War II, and it was still very racially divided. Archbishop Ritter took the courageous and just step of ordering the integration of all the schools in the Archdiocese of St. Louis. Many other bishops followed the lead of Archbishop Ritter. Thus, Catholic schools had eliminated the "separate but equal" system of education seven years before the U.S. Supreme Court ordered the integration of all government-controlled schools in *Brown v. Board of Education* (347 U.S. 483). So successful were the Catholic schools in achieving integration peacefully that three justices of the Supreme Court including Chief Justice Earl Warren visited Washington's Archbishop O'Boyle to seek his counsel on the integration of government-owned schools before the Court rendered its famous decision in 1954.

This historic act reinforced the commitment of Catholic schools to the education of all students. Today nearly 25 percent of the students in Catholic schools come from minority backgrounds and over 12 percent of the students are not members of the Catholic Church.

1965: Commitment to students

In this year, President Johnson signed the Elementary and Secondary Education Act which provided funds to assist students who were economically deprived and educationally disadvantaged. This legislation sought to help all children no matter what school they attended. Thus for the first time federal tax dollars were provided to assist students in Catholic schools. This concrete manifestation of the "child benefit theory" allowed many students to receive assistance in reading, mathematics, and English-as-a-second-language from teachers employed by the government-controlled schools. Initially this help was given in the Catholic school building and more recently it has had to be provided at a neutral site.

For almost thirty years Catholic school educators have worked under many trying circumstances with government education officials in order to secure assistance for their children. Perhaps more than any single event these thirty years of struggle and toil best manifest the deep concern that Catholic educators have for the individual and their desire to do all they can to help the student.

1972: Message, community, and service

In 1972, the American Catholic bishops approved their statement on Catholic education, *To Teach as Jesus Did*. In this the bishops clearly explained the three characteristics of Catholic education: message, community, and service. The bishops presented a clear rationale for Catholic education and described the philosophy upon which all Catholic educational institutions should be built. The bishops gave their highest praise to Catholic schools when they wrote: "Of the educational programs available to the Catholic community, Catholic schools afford the fullest and best opportunity to realize the threefold purpose of Christian education among children and young people" (no. 101). Of all the church documents on Catholic education, this one has probably had the most profound and lasting effect.

1991: Commitment to the future

In November of this year in the nation's capital, the National Catholic Educational Association held the National Congress: Catholic Schools for the 21st Century. This event was the culmination of more than a year of preparation during which over twenty-five regional meetings were held and over 5,000 members of the Catholic school community contributed ideas on the five themes: Catholic school identity; governance and finance; leadership of and on behalf of the schools; school and society; and public policy and political action. The 250 delegates to the Washington event developed directional statements for each of these five areas that presented a blueprint for leading schools into the next century. In early 1994 NCEA announced the follow-up to this meeting when it invited all Catholic schools to become an American Catholic School for the 21st Century.

Today, Catholic school educators prepare students for an unknown future. Notwithstanding past achievements, Catholic schools must be prepared to meet the challenges of each new student.

Conclusion

American Catholic schools have a long and rich history. They have taken millions of immigrants and turned them into productive citizens. They have been instrumental in making the Catholic Church in the United States one of the most successful in the world. These schools are truly a gift to the nation and a gift to the Church. They have been so successful because they have retained their philosophical commitment to the uniqueness of each individual and their determination to enable children to grow in a love of Jesus and the wonders of God's creation.

Reflection Questions

1. How does the Catholic school on a daily basis bring into harmony faith, culture, and life?

2. Some people say that Catholic schools only assist the more affluent child. How would you refute this argument?

3. Father Andrew Greeley (1992) has suggested that the clergy should remove themselves from Catholic schools and turn their governance over completely to the laity. Explain why you agree or disagree with him.

4. What is the role of religious women in Catholic education today?

5. Some people have criticized priests and bishops for not supporting Catholic schools. Why do you agree or disagree with this criticism based on the history of Catholic schools and on the experiences of today?

6. Some people advocate that the Catholic Church should remove itself from the education of children and concentrate on adults. How would you respond to this statement?

7. What are the essential ingredients in the education of a Catholic school teacher?

8. What does "parents are the first educators of their children" mean?

9. How has the Catholic school community reached out to various minority communities in the past and how is it doing this today?

10. Should Catholic schools accept government vouchers from parents? Explain your response.

11. As you reflect on the life of Jesus, what does it mean to teach as he did?

12. How will Catholic schools be different 50 years from now? What will never be different about them?

Resources

Buetow, H. A. 1988. *The Catholic school: Its roots, identity, and future.* New York: Crossroad Publishing Company.

Congregation for Catholic Education. 1988. *The religious dimension of education in a Catholic school: Guidelines for reflection and renewal.* Washington, D.C.: United States Catholic Conference.

Grant, M. A., and T. C. Hunt. 1992. *Catholic school education in the United States.* New York: Garland Publishing.

Greeley, A. M. 1992. A modest proposal for the reform of Catholic schools. Summarized in *National congress: Catholic schools for the 21st century: Executive summary*, eds. M. Guerra, R. Haney, and R. Kealy. Washington, D.C.: National Catholic Educational Association.

Guerra, M., R. Haney, and R. Kealey, eds. 1992. *National congress: Catholic schools for the 21st century: Executive summary.* Washington, D.C.: National Catholic Educational Association.

National Conference of Catholic Bishops. 1972. *To teach as Jesus did: A pastoral message on Catholic education.* Washington, D.C.: United States Catholic Conference.

————. 1990. *In support of Catholic elementary and secondary schools.* Washington, D.C.: United States Catholic Conference.

O'Brien, J. S. 1987. *Mixed messages: What bishops and priests say about Catholic schools.* Washington, D.C.: National Catholic Educational Association.

The author, Robert J. Kealey, Ed.D., is executive director of the Department of Elementary Schools for the National Catholic Educational Association in Washington, D.C.

The Principal as
EDUCATIONAL
LEADER
◆◆◆

O verview

If spiritual leadership gives "heart" or spirit to the Catholic school, then educational leadership provides the "head" or basic direction for the school program. The essence of Catholic schools involves a consistent mission, vision, and philosophy that shape the curriculum, instruction, and ultimately learning.

Affirming that "effective leadership is critical to the mission of the church and the future of Catholic schools" (p. 29), the *National Congress: Catholic Schools for the 21st Century: Executive Summary* (1992) presents several specific directional statements as standards for the educational leadership of Catholic school principals. Among them are

🙠 We demand that innovation, experimentation, risk taking, collaboration, and collegiality be the hallmarks of Catholic school leadership (p. 30).

🙠 We will champion superior standards of academic excellence (p. 18).

🙠 We commit ourselves to teach an integrated curriculum rooted in gospel values and Catholic teachings (p. 18).

Two types of responsibilities are encompassed in educational leadership. First, the principal must employ effective leadership behaviors to clearly articulate the vision and goals of the school. Second, the principal must oversee its curriculum and instruction.

LEADERSHIP

Frequently one hears the phrase, "Leadership makes the difference." The role of leader in a Catholic school goes beyond the generic definition, "the position or office of a leader." According to Ristau (1991), leaders are those who hold a strong belief about what needs to be done and why. They see ways to get things accomplished. They are risk takers with only a bit of sensible fear about the future. Fullan (1991) succinctly confirms this by stating that leadership relates to mission, direction, and inspiration.

As educational leader in a Catholic school, the principal is expected to demonstrate symbolic and cultural leadership skills, applying a Catholic educational vision to the daily activities of school life. The principal promotes healthy staff morale and recognizes and fosters leadership among staff members. Using research to guide action plans, the principal identifies and effects needed change. Finally, the principal attends to his or her own personal growth and professional development.

Helm provides a context for a model of Catholic school leadership reviewing the literature to explore how leadership has been studied. *A Leadership Perspective for Catholic Schools* (page 46) proposes that a transformational style of leadership most nearly embodies the ideals of the Catholic school.

CURRICULUM AND INSTRUCTION

Glatthorn (1987) defines **curriculum** in terms of the plans made for guiding learning. The plans are usually presented in the form of documents or charts. Curriculum and instruction, he maintains, are almost inseparable. **Instruction** is the curriculum as it is taught. One of the tasks of curriculum leadership is to use the right methods to more closely align the written and the taught curriculum.

The principal, in providing leadership in curriculum and instruction, must have a broadly developed set of understandings and skills. Heft (1991) notes that leaders of Catholic schools are expected to support a vision of achieving excellence in academics within the context of a community of faith. The Congregation for Catholic Education (*The Religious Dimension of Education in a Catholic School* 1988) emphasizes the necessity of infusing gospel values.

The principal as educational leader in a Catholic school is expected to understand the developmental stages of children and youth to appropriately integrate the content and methods of religious education and Christian values into the curriculum. To model respectfulness, the educational leader is expected to recognize and provide for cultural and religious differences in the ways the curriculum is presented.

In order to constructively supervise the instructional aspects of the school, the principal is expected to understand a variety of educational and pedagogical skills and to direct the faculty in developing inclusive instruction for all students. Since evaluation is an important component of educational improvement, the principal is expected to demonstrate an understanding of effective procedures for evaluating the learning of students and the general school program.

Innes' work, *Curriculum Components for Catholic Education* (page 62), presents a curriculum model for the consideration of Catholic educators. She proposes ten specific areas that, in the light of the distinctive mission of Catholic schools, call for particular consideration in developing a comprehensive Catholic school curriculum.

A *Leadership Perspective for Catholic Schools*

Claire M. Helm, Ph.D.

Where there is no vision, the people perish. (Prv 29:18)

If you can help them [faculty] meet needs, if you can inspire them to do it gladly, you are leading; if you are telling them, you're not leading! (Helm 1989, p. 148)

"When people ask me what I do all day, I say 'I walk around is what I do . . . and sometimes I think—at the end of the day—do I have anything to show for it?'" This admission by an experienced Catholic school principal (Helm 1989, p. 100) would not be surprising to most veteran administrators. What usually stuns new principals is, in fact, the sheer scope and complexity of the typical job description for the principal. After looking at a proposed checklist of the principal's responsibilities, one would-be administrator groaned and exclaimed, "I do wonder if the Lord himself could do this job!"

Thus the common question facing Catholic school administrators is "What should be the primary focus of the Catholic school principal?" or, put another way, "What do I need to do myself and what should I delegate?" The answer to this simple but critical question is rooted in a thorough understanding of leadership theory and a deep appreciation for the unique mission of the Catholic school.

In search of leaders

A trip through the dense forest of leadership literature to the present interest in cultural and symbolic leadership requires more than a compass. Few authors are able to agree even on a definition of leadership (Stogdill 1974). Yukl (1981) notes that "The most commonly used measure of leader effectiveness is the extent to which the leader's group or organization performs its task successfully and attains its goals" (p. 5). Kellerman (1984) asserts that leadership is "getting people to follow" (p. ix).

Regardless of the definition favored, most agree that leadership is at the heart of the successful organization. So from Galton's (1870) "great man" theory to Roberts' (1985) light-hearted summary of the leadership secrets of Attila the Hun, scholars and researchers have searched for clues to identify effective leaders. Research on leadership in the formal sense, however, is less than a century old (Stogdill 1974). Yukl (1981) notes that most of the research on leadership can be classified according to one of the following approaches: 1) trait, 2) behavior, 3) situational/contingency, and 4) power/influence.

Trait studies

One of the earliest attempts to study leadership used the trait approach. Leaders were thought to possess certain traits not found in others. The focus of most preliminary studies was the comparison of leaders with nonleaders with respect to physical characteristics, personality, and ability. This initial research did not surface traits that appeared to correlate with leadership effectiveness. Yukl (1981) asserts that this line of research tended to treat the factors "in an atomistic fashion, suggesting that each trait acted singly to determine leadership effects" (Stogdill 1974, p. 82). Hollander (1985) pointed out that the relationship of the leader to the situation was neglected as a relevant factor in these studies.

Later research used more relevant traits and improved measures and focused on patterns rather than isolated traits and skills. This later approach suggests that certain general characteristics can differentiate leaders from followers (Yukl 1981). For example an important predictor of managerial success is the broad category of managerial motivation, in particular, the desire to exercise power, a drive to compete with peers, and a positive attitude toward authority figures (McClelland 1975, Miner 1978).

Stogdill (1974) summarized trait research by noting that the characteristics of effective leaders could be grouped into *task*-related traits, such as the need for achievement, enterprise, and initiative, and *social* traits, such as the ability to enlist support, cooperation, and nurturance. Along with studies highlighting the importance of the motivational patterns of leaders, Katz (1955) and Mann (1965) focused their attention on the three types of skills associated with all effective leaders:

- human relations skills (e.g., the ability to communicate clearly and effectively),
- technical skills (e.g., specialized knowledge of methods and procedures), and
- conceptual skills (e.g., problem-solving ability).

Behavior studies

Studies of leader behavior have been both popular and useful (Yukl 1981), but the lack of agreement across studies and "the absence of a widely accepted taxonomy" of leader behaviors are "disturbing" (p. 120). Some of the earliest studies of effective and ineffective leader behaviors were done through the Ohio State Leadership Studies organized in 1945. Items on the Leader Behavior Description Questionnaire (LBDQ) yielded two patterns of behavior of particular interest. *Consideration* behavior was helpfulness, friendliness, and availability to subordinates. *Initiating structure* behavior was getting subordinates to follow rules and maintaining performance standards.

Stogdill (1974) concluded that research on the relationship of these two factors (consideration and initiation) to group productivity, satisfaction, and cohesiveness has been positive. "The most effective leaders tend to be described as high on both scales" (Stogdill 1974, p. 394). However, Yukl (1981) points out, "[T]he more general a behavior category is, . . . the less useful it is for determining what makes a leader effective in a particular situation" (p. 120).

In addition to the use of questionnaires such as the LBDQ, leader behavior has been studied using observation, activity sampling, self-report diaries, interviews, and the use of the critical incident (Yukl 1981). Efforts to develop a useful taxonomy that reconciles the discrepancies of earlier studies continue even today. Yukl and Nemeroff's (1979) list of nineteen discriminating leader behaviors includes the following:

- emphasis on subordinate performance,
- consideration given to subordinates,
- inspiration provided by the leader,
- planning by the leader,
- the management of conflict,
- the training of subordinates, and
- the extent to which praise and recognition is offered.

Situational/contingency studies

Situational theories of leadership assume that different situations require different patterns of traits and behaviors for a leader to be effective. Situational theories underscored the need to identify the factors or "moderator variables" that enhanced or nullified the influence of a leader's traits, skills, or behavior (Yukl 1981). The variables to be considered are the task itself and the past history, culture, norms, and size of the group (Hollander 1985). Situational theories have been studied by several researchers including

ِ&ـ Fiedler's Contingency Model (1964),
ِ&ـ Hershey and Blanchard's Situational Theory (1977),
ِ&ـ House's Path Goal Theory (1971),
ِ&ـ Vroom and Yetton's Decision-Making Model (1973), and
ِ&ـ Yukl's Multiple Linkage Model of Leadership (1981).

These theories are similar in that each deals with the effects of leaders on the satisfaction, motivation, and performance of subordinates.

Hollander (1985) notes that Fiedler's Contingency Model of Leadership Effectiveness has helped "to bridge the trait and situational approaches and opened the way for other useful contingency concepts" (p. 499). Yukl (1981) summarized his analysis of situational theories of leadership by concluding that they are "complex, imprecisely formulated, and difficult to test" (p. 169).

Power/influence studies

The fourth major approach to the study of leadership, that of power/influence, attempts to explain leader effectiveness in terms of the source of power, whether position or personality, or amount of power available to leaders and the manner in which leaders exercise power or influence over followers. Power/influence research has also attempted to identify the impact of subordinates on leaders.

One of the most prominent power/influence theories is the Social Exchange Theory which examined the reciprocal influence between leaders and subordinates. According to this theory a fundamental form of social interaction is an exchange of benefits or favors which over time contributes to expectations of rewards (Yukl 1981). Leaders and followers both achieve their separate purposes because each has something perceived to be valuable or needed by the other. This "valuable" is used as a "bargaining chip" to satisfy the other's need. This theory is usually called upon to explain one-to-one interactions.

How leaders use power in situations where there are several subordinates is another focus of research. French and Raven (1959) propose a particularly useful topology to explain the uses of power (Yukl 1981). This topology identifies five sources of power for a leader:

    ⬇ reward power: the subordinate does something in order to be rewarded;

- coercive power: the subordinate does something to avoid punishment;
- legitimate power: the leader is acknowledged to have the right or authority;
- expert power: the leader is perceived to have special knowledge or skills; and
- referent power: the subordinate admires and tends to identify with the leader.

McClelland (1970) asserts that leaders can use any of these types of power in two ways: to dominate—keeping subordinates dependent—or to empower—building the skills and confidence of subordinates. Yukl (1981) observes that historically, charismatic leaders often employ a blend of uplifting and domineering power in their leadership. This has had both good (Gandhi) and disastrous (Hitler) effects. Since almost all leadership entails some degree of charisma, the concept is worthy of our further study.

Charisma, according to Weber (1947) is applied "to a certain quality of an individual's personality by virtue of which he [*sic*] is set apart from ordinary men [*sic*] and treated as endowed with supernatural, superhuman, or at least specifically exceptional powers or qualities" (p. 358). House (1977) first summarized the effects of charismatic leadership on followers as

- causing followers to model their behavior, affect, and beliefs after their leaders;
- articulating a transcendent goal or mission for the followers;
- inspiring self-confidence in the followers; and
- bringing about some change in the status quo.

House (1977) hypothesized that charismatic leaders behave in ways that set them apart from other leaders. Such behaviors include

- role modeling of a specific value system for the follower;
- goal articulation, particularly of a futuristic or transcendent nature (e.g., Martin Luther King's "I Have a Dream" speech);
- demonstration of confidence and high expectations for others; and
- motive-arousal leader behavior which refers to the behaviors that arouse motives in followers related to the accomplishment of the goal or mission.

Although there are some serious methodological limitations in the power studies (Yukl 1981), there have also been some significant findings for leaders. Effective leaders tend to rely more on their personal power (e.g., helping behavior) rather than their position power (e.g., insistence on proper titles) even though both types are necessary (Whyte 1969).

Stogdill (1974) uses the word "bewildering" (p. vii) to summarize his assessment of the leadership research. Yukl (1981) notes that while the field is presently in a "state of ferment and confusion" (p. 268), progress has been made in the development of our understanding of leadership processes and in the identification of the determinants of leadership effectiveness. He highlights three approaches for the improvement of leadership:

- an emphasis on research-based selection processes,
- training for effectiveness, and
- situation engineering which involves changing the situation to be more compatible with the leader's strengths.

A new paradigm of leadership

As this brief summary of the literature concludes, the study of leadership is neither straightforward nor simple. A glance at recent titles related to leadership effectiveness makes it evident that the last word on leadership has yet to be written! Many of the recent paradigms of leadership study the dynamic involved in leader-follower interactions. Burns (1978) argued that it was time to bring the literature on leadership and the literature on followership together. He asserts that there are two kinds of leadership: one transactional and the other transformational in nature.

Transactional leadership occurs when one person makes contact with another for the purpose of exchanging something of value or to satisfy personal needs (Burns 1978). It recognizes what it is we want from our work and attempts to provide it based on the performance given (Bass 1985). Transactional leadership responds to the subordinate's immediate self-interests. It is thus a reciprocal relationship in which both the leader and the subordinate exert influence or power over one another. It has many overtones of exchange theory. Bass (1985) argued, however, that a purely transactional or exchange approach to leadership was not enough to explain all types of leadership. For instance it would not explain the leadership of a Winston Churchill or a Lee Iacocca.

Burns (1978) suggests that transformational leadership recognizes the immediate needs and demands of followers but also seeks to satisfy higher needs and engages the "full person of the follower" (p. 4). The result is a kind of moral leadership because it "elevates" both the follower and the leader through a "mutual stimulation" to a "new awareness about issues of consequence" (Bass

1985, p. 17). This type of leadership embodies many of the characteristics of charismatic leadership.

Burns (1978) pointed to the significance of transformational leadership when he said, "I define leadership as leaders inducing followers to act for certain goals that represent the values and motivations—the wants and needs, the aspirations and expectations—of both leader and followers" (p. 19). Transformational leadership in the words of Bass (1985) is "leadership that motivates followers to work for transcendental goals and for aroused higher-level needs for self-actualization rather than for immediate self-interest" (p. 11). Bass maintains that this form of leadership results in achievement of higher levels of performance among individuals than previously thought possible.

The Catholic school has a mission orientation that integrates religious and academic purposes. The leader in this context must possess a strong faith and firm allegiance to the goals of the Catholic Church which is combined with an unshakable conviction about the potency of an excellent education. It appears that the characteristics of a transformational leadership style are an appropriate "fit" for one charged with preserving the integrity of the Catholic school mission. The seminal work of such researchers and writers as House (1977), Burns (1978), Bennis (1984), Bass (1985), and Sergiovanni (1990, 1992) all speak to values and expectations held for Catholic school leadership. Transcendental goals, the emphasis on value-added leadership, moral leadership, and servant leadership (Sergiovanni 1992)—the language of transformational leaders—is all quite compatible with the traditions and desires of Catholic school leaders in this country.

School effectiveness and the culture of the school

Before turning our attention to the unique environment that is the Catholic school, the next stop on the journey to understanding the demands on leadership in Catholic schools is to examine the institution to be led. A brief review of the growing body of research now popularly termed "school effectiveness research" will give form to the responsibilities of the Catholic school principal.

Some troubling reports on U.S. public education (e.g., *A Nation at Risk: The Imperative for Educational Reform* [United States Department of Education 1983]), helped to spawn the search for effective school practices as well as the leadership that contributes to this success. The research indicates that, despite socioeconomic differences, effective schools share common characteristics:

- strong instructional leadership;
- high expectations for student achievement;
- well-defined goals, in particular, a strong academic program;
- local control over instruction and staff inservice programs;
- a safe, orderly environment;
- a cohesive approach to discipline;
- a system of monitoring student progress; and
- regular student attendance (Edmonds 1979, Purkey and Smith 1982).

Attempts to understand how the characteristics of effective schools influence student learning have provided current researchers with a fascinating agenda. Briefly, the findings note that a school, as an institution, possesses a climate which permeates all aspects of school life. Describing precisely the nature of climate is often challenging. An oft-used example of the presence of climate is that a visitor walking into a school will get a "feel" for the place. This intuitive reaction is noted more objectively by Tagiuri (1968), who described climate as the total environmental quality within the school. He proposed it had four dimensions: ecology, milieu, social systems, and culture. Ecology is manifested in the physical aspects of the school such as the amount and type of student work or religious symbolism evident in the school. The milieu or social dimension includes teacher morale. The social systems incorporate the teacher-principal relationships. Finally, the culture encompasses the school's belief systems, values, cognitive structures, and meanings.

Deal and Kennedy (1983) state that culture is "the way we do things around here" (p. 14). For example, school people, whether children or adults, often try to adjust to a situation by conforming or fitting in. They "learn the ropes" by observing how others successfully maneuver in a situation and frequently follow suit with similar behavior. Put more formally, Deal (1987) asserts that those in school acquire a learned pattern of unconscious or semiconscious thought which is reflected in beliefs and reinforced by behavior. Culture then becomes embedded in the history, values, legends, stories, and ceremonies of the school and shapes the experiences of those associated with it.

Deal and Kennedy (1983) state that strong school cultures go hand in hand with school improvement. Strong cultures provide a bonding spirit that helps "teachers to teach; students to learn; and for parents, administrators, and others to contribute to the instructional process." Culture provides ways schools can communicate their identity to outside groups "through shared values, heroes and heroines, and rituals" (p. 15). To summarize: the school as an organization exudes a climate/culture that in turn affects student outcomes, behaviors, values, growth, and satisfaction (Anderson 1982).

Leadership and the Catholic school

Drawing on the work of Burns (1978) and the effective schools literature, leadership that attends to the unique culture and symbolism as part of a transformational style should ensure a school environment that embodies the characteristics of effective schools. In a Catholic school environment the administrator is challenged to develop a school climate that demonstrates the characteristics of effective schools but that is influenced and shaped by the values and beliefs of Catholicism. Thus Catholic school principals are challenged to be transformational leaders who are also cultural and symbolic.

A symbolic leader takes on the role of "chief." By emphasizing selective attention and modeling important goals through behaviors, the chief (leader) signals to others what is of importance and value (Sergiovanni 1984). "Purposing" is of major concern to the symbolic leader. Vaill (1984) defines purposing to be those "actions . . . which have the effect of inducing clarity, consensus, and commitment regarding the organization's basic purposes" (p. 91).

The cultural leader is portrayed as a "high priest" by Sergiovanni (1984). "Seeking to define, strengthen, and articulate those enduring values, beliefs, and cultural strands that give the school its unique identity" (p. 9) is the role of the high priest. The result of successful cultural leadership is the bonding together of students, teachers, and others as "believers in the work of the school" (p. 9).

Sergiovanni (1984) in his earlier writing specifies three functions necessary for the competent public school principal:

- the technical or sound management function,
- the human or interpersonal function, and
- the educational or instructional function.

More recently Sergiovanni (1992) has come to appreciate and emphasize a fourth dimension: fostering the cultural and symbolic aspects of the school. Attention to this latter dimension is essential in a complete Catholic education that encompasses both a religious and an academic purpose.

The specific mission of the Catholic school is "the critical, systematic transmission of culture in the light of faith and the bringing forth of the power of Christian virtue by the integration of culture with faith and of faith with living" (*The Catholic School* 1977, p. 119).

What might the Catholic school visitor experience that would distinguish this school and its "culture" from its public- or private-school neighbor? The authors of *The Religious Dimension of Education in a Catholic School* (Congregation for Catholic Education 1988, no. 25) express the hope that from "the first moment that a student sets foot into a Catholic school, he or she ought to have the impression of entering a new environment, one illumined by the light of faith, . . . having its own unique characteristics" and "permeated by the Gospel spirit of love and freedom."

Byrk, Holland, Lee, and Carriedo (1984) in their study of effective Catholic elementary schools made reference to the "distinctive character that transcends religious programs and personnel" (p. 15). This character was reflected in the perceptions of the school community about the religious purpose of the Catholic school, in the social interactions among faculty and students, and in the description by teachers of their role as ministers within the Church.

In *Evangelizing the Unconverted*, O'Malley (1991) contends that at the secondary level the challenge facing the administrators and mostly lay faculties of today is to continue to find ways to "evangelize the baptized but unconverted," "to discomfit the comfy," and to challenge the assumption of many adolescents that because they are "nice" they are necessarily good Christians (p. 3). The counter-cultural message of the Gospel in other words means that Catholic schools must continue to find ways to communicate the difficult truths of Christianity: its insecurity, apostleship, service, and suffering as well as an understanding of the Church as the "living presence of Jesus Christ in the world" (Heft 1991, p. 21).

McDermott (1985) categorized the four roles of the Catholic school leader as manager, academic leader, creator of the school environment, and religious leader. As academic leaders Catholic school principals must first seek not only "co-workers in the apostolate of teaching" (p. 43) with the appropriate credentials but also those who are going to participate as role models in the building of a Christian community. As creators of the school's climate or environment, principals are in the best position to provide the leadership necessary to create the unique sense of purpose, mission, and identity Sergiovanni (1984) claims is the mark of the truly excellent school. As religious leaders, "activators of the school's apostolic mission," Catholic school principals ensure that "growth in faith is central to the program of the school" . . . (and they summon) "the school's community to worship—the highest form of human activity" (McDermott, p. 45).

Observations of four Catholic elementary school principals, identified as transformational using Bass's Multifactor Leadership Questionnaire (Helm 1989), revealed that these principals appeared to use every opportunity to focus attention on the primacy of the school's purpose. Some of the strategies employed to this end were

- their example of practicing (modeling) as well as "preaching" the values espoused by the school,
- careful selection of teachers who "fit in" with their vision of what the school should be,
- reiteration of high expectations of the teachers as role models, and
- the emphasis placed on the central place occupied by religion class and religious services.

High visibility by the principal, attention paid to religious symbolism, and the high priority placed on positive teacher-principal and parent-principal relationships were also characteristic of all four administrators despite differences in personality and leadership style. Efforts to involve teachers in decision making appeared to contribute significantly to the high morale and positive climate apparent in these schools. Frequent, positive feedback and regular communication with teachers and parents were reflected in the high degree of cohesiveness of values identified as central to each school's mission. "The bottom line," as one teacher explained, "is that Christian values, witness, and religion are central to everything" (Helm 1989, p. 203).

Catholic school leaders for the 21st century

The answer to what should be the primary focus of a Catholic school principal thus lies in a thorough understanding and appreciation of the unique role of the Catholic school administrator. It begins with an understanding of the specific mission which is at the heart of the Catholic school: the integration of religious truth and values with life. Nurturing the dual purpose of providing an effective religious education with a quality academic education is the particular responsibility and charge of the Catholic school leader. In responding to this challenge the principal is the champion and protector of the Catholic identity of the school.

Effective principals have a clear understanding of the impact of a school's culture. More importantly, they must possess an acute awareness that as trustees of the school's identity they are in the focal position to provide the leadership necessary to create the special sense of purpose, mission, and identity that Sergiovanni (1984) claimed is the mark of the truly excellent school. This leadership is best described as cultural and symbolic or transformational. Catholic school leaders must exercise an educational vision that flows from the Catholic identity of the school and is respectful of its dual purpose. By promoting healthy staff morale and developing the leadership potential of the faculty, the Catholic school principal sustains the vision and strengthens the culture of the school. Identifying areas of needed change and developing action plans that are consistent with research are ways the leader preserves the mission and refreshes the school's identity.

It is not unusual for new principals as well as the "veterans" to express anxiety at the apparently formidable agenda facing them, particularly with respect to their religious leadership role. The words and actions of Jesus offer their own challenge as well as model. Jesus called a little child to stand in the midst of the disciples and, putting his arms around the child, Jesus said to the disciples: "Whoever welcomes a child such as this for my sake, welcomes me. And whoever welcomes me, welcomes not me, but him who sent me" (Mk 9:37). And in another place, Jesus said: "Let the children come to me and do not hinder them. It is to just such as these that the kingdom of God belongs" (Mk 10:14). Principals also could recall that Jesus clearly said: "It was not you who chose me, it was I who chose you to go forth and bear fruit. Your fruit must endure so that all you ask the Father in my name he will give you. The command I give you is this, that you love one another" (Jn 15:16–17).

U.S. Catholic school leaders of the twenty-first century inherit the legacy of all those who have gone before them—a legacy and rich tradition embedded in the histories of our schools and in the biographies of the clergy and the religious men and women whose faith, courage, and vision nurtured and inspired us all. May their legacy live on in the next generation of leaders!

Reflection Questions

1. Some say "leaders are born not made." What conclusions do you draw after reviewing the leadership literature?

2. Are there any specific personal traits needed to function effectively in the particular context of Catholic education?

3. What, if any, particular behaviors are expected of Catholic school leaders by the parish? parents? civic community? public school counterparts?

4. Much of the literature specifies that the "situation" must be taken into account when examining the effectiveness of the leader. Catholic schools serve diverse communities nationwide that have widely divergent economic conditions, resources, and needs. How do the particular circumstances of a school community influence the leadership of the Catholic school principal?

5. Because most of the administration of the Catholic school is decided and managed at the local school level (in contrast to the more centralized public school system), the Catholic school principal has a broad scope of responsibilities. Emerging needs such as the necessity for systematic public relations, marketing, development programs, political action demands, and the family's expanding child care needs further tax the resources of the school and its personnel. In the face of these formidable obligations how ought the Catholic school principal proceed?

6. In the Catholic school context is it more appropriate for the principal to rely on "personal" or "position" power to effect change?

7. Practically speaking, in the overall leadership context of the Catholic school, are there any characteristics of a transactional style versus a transformational style that Catholic school leaders might emphasize in order to achieve the dual purpose of the Catholic school?

8. How would you apply the cultural and symbolic behavior of leaders theoretically presented in this chapter to a specific Catholic school familiar to you?

9. Keeping in mind the expectations of the Catholic school principal: What if any, aspects of leadership must ordinarily be reserved to the principal or head of the school? Which aspects are more appropriately shared?

Resources

Anderson, C. S. 1982. The search for school climate: A review of the research. *Review of Educational Research* 52(3):368–420.

Bass, B. M. 1985. Leadership and performance beyond expectations. New York: The Free Press.

Bennis, W. 1984. Transformation power and leadership. In *Leadership and organizational culture*, ed. T. J. Sergiovanni and J. E. Corbally, 64–71. Urbana-Champaign: University of Illinois Press.

Bryk, A. S., P. B. Holland, V. E. Lee, and R. A. Carriedo. 1984. *Effective Catholic schools: An exploration.* Washington, D.C.: National Catholic Educational Association.

Burns, J. M. 1978. *Leadership.* New York: Harper and Row.

Congregation for Catholic Education. 1977. *The Catholic school.* Washington, D.C.: United States Catholic Conference.

———. 1988. *The religious dimension of education in a Catholic school: Guidelines for reflection and renewal.* Washington, D.C.: United States Catholic Conference.

Deal, T. E. 1987. The culture of schools. In *Leadership: Examining the elusive, 1987 Yearbook*, 3–15. Alexandria, Va.: Association for Supervision and Curriculum Development.

Deal, T. E., and A. A. Kennedy. 1983. Culture and school performance. *Educational Leadership* 40(5):14–15.

Deal, T. E. and K. D. Peterson. 1990. *The principal's role in shaping school culture.* Washington, D.C.: United States Department of Education.

Drahmann, T., and A. Stenger. 1989. *The Catholic school principal: An outline for action.* Revised. Washington, D.C.: National Catholic Educational Association.

Edmonds, R. R. 1979. Effective schools for the urban poor. *Educational Leadership* 37(2):15–27.

Fiedler, F. E. 1964. A contingency model of leadership effectiveness. In *Advances in experimental social psychology*, ed. L. Berkowitz. New York: Academic Press.

French, J. R., and B. Raven. 1959. The bases of social power. In *Studies in social power*, ed. D. Cartwright. Ann Arbor, Mich.: Institute for Social Research.

Galton, F. 1870. *Hereditary genius.* New York: Appleton.

Heft, J. 1991. Catholic identity and the Church. In *What makes a Catholic school Catholic?*, ed. F. D. Kelly, 14–21. Washington, D.C.: National Catholic Educational Association.

Helm, C. M. 1989. Cultural and symbolic leadership in Catholic elementary schools: An ethnographic study. Ph.D. diss., The Catholic University of America, Washington, D.C.

Hersey, P., and K. H. Blanchard. 1977. *Management of organizational behavior.* 3d ed. Englewood Cliffs, N.J.: Prentice-Hall.

Hollander, E. P. 1985. Leadership and power. In *Handbook of social psychology.* Vol. II. *Special fields and applications*, ed. E. Aronson, 3d ed., 485–537. New York: Random House.

House, R. J. 1971. A path goal theory of leader effectiveness. *Administrative Science Quarterly* 16:321–39.

————. 1977. A 1976 theory of charismatic leadership. In *Leadership: The cutting edge*, ed. J. G. Hunt and L. L. Larson, 189–207. Carbondale: Southern Illinois University Press.

Katz, R. L. 1955. Skills of an effective administrator. *Harvard Business Review* January-February: 33–42.

Kellerman, B., ed. 1984. *Leadership: Multidisciplinary perspectives.* Englewood Cliffs, N.J.: Prentice-Hall.

Kelly, F. D., ed. 1991. *What makes a Catholic school Catholic?* Washington, D.C.: National Catholic Educational Association.

Larranaga, R. 1990. *Calling it a day: Daily meditations for workaholics.* San Francisco: Harper and Row.

Mann, F. C. 1965. Toward an understanding of the leadership role in formal organization. In *Leadership and productivity*, ed. R. Dubin, G. C. Homans, F. C. Mann, and D. C. Miller. San Francisco: Chandler.

McClelland, D. 1970. The two faces of power. *Journal of International Affairs* 24(1):29–47.

————. 1975. *Power: The inner experience.* New York: Irvington.

McDermott, E. 1985. Distinctive qualities of the Catholic school. In *NCEA Keynote Series No. 1.* Washington, D.C.: National Catholic Educational Association.

Miner, J. B. 1978. Twenty years of research on role motivation theory of managerial effectiveness. *Personnel Psychology* 31:739–60.

Nouwen, H. 1989. *In the name of Jesus: Reflections on Christian leadership.* New York: Crossroad Publishing Company.

O'Malley, W. J. 1991. Evangelizing the unconverted. In *What makes a Catholic school Catholic?*, ed. F. D. Kelly, 3–9. Washington, D.C.: National Catholic Educational Association.

Purkey, S., and M. S. Smith. 1982. Synthesis of research on effective schools. *Educational Leadership* 40(3):64–69.

Roberts, W. 1985. *Leadership secrets of Attila the Hun.* New York: Warner Books.

Sergiovanni, T. J. 1984. Leadership and excellence in schooling. *Educational Leadership* 41(5):4–13.

————. 1990. *Value-added leadership: How to get extraordinary performance in schools.* San Diego: Harcourt, Brace, Jovanovich Publishers.

————. 1992. *Moral leadership: Getting to the heart of school improvement.* San Francisco: Jossey-Bass Publishers.

Stogdill, R. M. 1974. *Handbook of leadership: A survey of theory and research.* New York: The Free Press.

Tagiuri, R. 1968. The concept of organizational climate. In *Organizational climate: Exploration of a concept*, ed. R. Tagiuri and G. H. Litwin. Boston: Harvard University, Division of Research, Graduate School of Business Administration.

United States Department of Education. 1983. *A nation at risk: The imperative for educational reform.* Washington, D.C.

Vaill, P. B. 1984. The purposing of high-performing systems. In *Leadership and organizational culture*, ed. T. J. Sergiovanni and J. E. Corbally, 85–104. Urbana-Champaign: University of Illinois Press.

Vroom, V. H., and P. W. Yetton. 1973. *Leadership and decision-making.* Pittsburgh: University of Pittsburgh Press.

Weber, M. 1947. *The theory of social and economic organization.* New York: Oxford University Press.

Whyte, W. F. 1969. *Organizational behavior: Theory and applications.* Homewood, Ill.: Irwin.

Yukl, G. A. 1981. *Leadership in organizations.* Englewood Cliffs, N.J.: Prentice-Hall, Inc.

Yukl, G. A., and W. Nemeroff. 1979. Identification and measurement of specific categories of leadership behavior: A progress report. In *Crosscurrents in leadership*, ed. J. G. Hunt and L. L. Larson. Cardondale: Southern Illinois University Press.

The author, Claire M. Helm, Ph.D., is president of the Academy of Holy Names in Tampa, Florida.

Curriculum Components for Catholic Education

Sr. Donna Innes, CSA, Ph.D.

The National Conference of Catholic Bishops of the United States explicitly states that "the educational efforts of the" Church must encompass the twin purposes of personal sanctification and social reform in light of Christian values (*To Teach as Jesus Did* 1972, p. 3). Thus, the Catholic school has a clear mandate from its institution, the Catholic Church, to instill values into the curriculum of the school and to work with parents to create a community that fosters the acquisition of values within the child. Imparting values, while allowing for the free will and the development of the student's conscience, is central to the mission of the Catholic school. The curriculum is the major vehicle by which this mission is achieved.

The curriculum of the Catholic school takes on unique characteristics because religious values are integrated with human values. As the curriculum addresses the spiritual, moral, physical, intellectual, emotional, social, and aesthetic development of the students, it enfleshes the school philosophy. The curriculum reflects Catholic beliefs, develops the student's responsibility to self, home, community, and the world, and includes a sensitivity to social justice and global peace concerns, while always being mindful that "the ultimate goal of all Catholic education is salvation in Jesus Christ" (*The Catholic School of the '80s* 1987, no. 8).

In light of the distinctive mission of Catholic schools, the following ten areas require careful deliberation when developing a comprehensive curriculum:

- philosophy;
- family, church, state/nation (background influences);
- global vision/world view;
- policies, guidelines, goals, and objectives;
- instructional strategies that apply appropriate learning theory;
- staff development;
- content (scope and sequence);
- instructional materials;
- systematic and periodic assessment/evaluation;
- an ongoing curriculum assessment cycle.

Philosophy

Through the clear articulation of its philosophy and by meeting definite curriculum standards, Catholic schools manifest "a clear sense of their identity and the courage to follow all the consequences of their uniqueness." (*The Catholic School* 1977, no. 66). The Catholic theology and philosophy of education that permeates the Catholic school forms the basis on which each of the other nine elements of the curriculum model are based.

A Catholic school curriculum model must recognize the individual as empowered by God, an individual with freedom and dignity. It must address beliefs and values to be inculcated through the MESSAGE element of the curriculum, augmented through WORSHIP occasions, supported through the COMMUNITY, and manifested in SERVICE opportunities (*Sharing the Light of Faith* 1979). Values to be imparted in the Catholic school include

> affection, respect, obedience, gratitude, gentleness, goodness, helpful-
> ness, service and good example [as well as] a love for all that excludes
> no one because of religion, nationality or race; prayer for all, so that
> all may know God; laboring together in apostolic works and in efforts
> to relieve human suffering; a preferential option for the less fortunate,
> the sick, the poor, the handicapped, the lonely (*The Religious Dimension
> of Education in a Catholic School* 1988, no. 87).

Family, church, state/nation

Each individual lives within the context of the social forces of society. These social forces include the family, the Church and the local parish, the local community, and the community-at-large in the state and nation. The curriculum of a Catholic school needs to assist each individual in identifying how the social forces of society can be balanced with gospel beliefs and values.

The intrinsic right of parents to educate their children is clearly acknowledged by the Catholic Church (*Declaration on Christian Education* 1966, no. 6, *The Religious Dimension of Education in a Catholic School,* no. 43). When the Catholic school integrates the fullness of Christ's message into the total curriculum and includes parents in the design, implementation, and evaluation of the curriculum, it supports parents in their responsibilities toward their children.

All members of the Catholic school community are called upon to develop an environment in which the curriculum and instruction appropriate for a

Catholic school can challenge students and impart gospel values. A sense of community is created within the school as parents, students, administrators, teachers, staff, clergy, and parishioners witness to the Gospel in their lives and support each other. In such an environment students are influenced and come to understand "the meaning of [their] faith experiences and their truths" (*The Catholic School* no. 27). Thus in a successful Catholic school the people involved with the school and the sharing of values through the curriculum merge to create a meaningful school climate.

Global vision/worldview

The need to assist students in developing a global vision and world view is based on the two preceding areas: the philosophical core and the relationship of the individual to the family and to society. This phase of a good curriculum model focuses on the Gospel message and considers the cultural conditions of the times (*The Catholic School* no. 9).

Creating a global vision is a difficult task. However, this task is made easier in Catholic education because of the belief in the dignity of each person which is integral to the Gospel message of Jesus. When this basic integrity is applied to each human being in all of creation, multicultural understanding and a sense of oneness or universality becomes an essential part of the curriculum.

A global vision/world view can only be a true part of the curriculum when it is possessed by teachers, administrators, and parents and when it is consciously incorporated into all aspects of the curriculum.

Policies, guidelines, goals, and objectives

In the process of curriculum development, the procedures for assessing needs and for setting goals and objectives are tools used to facilitate the ongoing development of the curriculum. Here the curriculum process moves from its philosophical base to its implementation, i.e., from theory to practice.

Curriculum implementation occurs best when policies are established and clearly recognized by the school community.

The policies and guidelines for the curriculum need to be the connection links from the philosophical base of the curriculum to the applied theory of contact areas.

The goals and objectives of the curriculum should reflect the philosophy and policies of the school and be in harmony with gospel values. The total curriculum, composed of each of the content areas, should recognize the needs of each student and interact appropriately with the content of the total curriculum.

Instructional strategies/learning theory

The faculty of the school makes learning theory a reality as they apply it in the curriculum. Through staff development, teachers can consistently be updated in current learning theories. As teachers become knowledgeable about learning styles and apply teaching strategies appropriate to the individual student, they bridge the education gap from theory to practice.

Staff development

The importance of teachers in transmitting the Christian message, not only through the curriculum but also by their whole being, is reiterated in each of the church documents on Catholic education. *Lay Catholics in Schools: Witnesses to Faith* (1982) states unequivocally that in the future it will be lay teachers who will substantially determine whether or not the school realizes its aims and accomplishes its objectives. Teachers are challenged to live and reflect the Christian message of Christ; to integrate religious truth, values, culture, and faith in their own lives; and to understand the mission and uniqueness of the Catholic school (*The Catholic School* nos. 43, 66; *To Teach as Jesus Did* no. 104). Teachers' attitudes about life influence the decisions they make. Therefore, the identity of the teacher has a great influence upon the school, curriculum, and students. The Catholic school teacher must not only be an educator, but also a model of the values promoted by the school.

Content (scope and sequence)

The scope and sequence of learning objectives should provide the student with necessary and appropriate information and skills and must integrate gospel values and the teachings of the Catholic Church into the content areas. When such integration occurs, the Catholic school is successful.

The scope and sequence, as one area of curriculum development, not only concentrate on theory and skills for specific subject areas such as religion, language arts (reading, writing, and speaking), mathematics, science, social studies, music, art, physical education, health, foreign languages, and especially religion, but they also must recognize and impart gospel (religious) values relevant to the content area (*The Catholic School of the '80s* no. 7).

Students need processes and procedures that will enable them to think, to plan, to cooperate, and to act by their own decisions. Learning how to learn, understanding one's own world view, knowing how to plan, being able to create one's own environment, knowing oneself and one's own values, as well as understanding how to interact with others—all are curriculum goals for today's world (Hanlon 1973).

Instructional materials

The quality and type of instructional materials used in the Catholic school should reflect the teaching of the Catholic Church and the philosophy of the school. They should meet the needs of the students and enable them to learn properly the content and skills of the curriculum. These materials include not only textbooks but also manipulative materials, maps, globes, charts, science equipment, games, audiovisual equipment, calculators, library books, computers, and computer software. The instructional materials augment the scope and sequence and the learning objectives of the curriculum.

Periodic assessment/evaluation

Evaluation needs to occur at every level of the curriculum. Ongoing evaluation is called formative evaluation. At the completion of a course, project, or activity, it is important to have a structured summative evaluation.

An achievement-testing program is one source of summative evaluation. However, standardized testing programs have several limitations; therefore, other types of student assessment are needed to evaluate the spiritual, cognitive, affective, and psycho-motor growth of the students.

Ongoing curriculum assessment

Curriculum planning needs to be systematic. Curriculum development is an ongoing process and having a long-range curriculum plan allows the school a consistency in curriculum planning. The curriculum of any Catholic school needs to be centered on the message of Christ as reflected in Scripture and through the teaching of the Church. A cyclical plan for curriculum development includes the review and assessment of philosophy, policies, guidelines, goals and objectives, scope and sequence of subject areas, instructional strategies, staff development, instructional materials, testing program, quality of parent involvement, and the impact of current social forces.

A Catholic school is successful when students possess the knowledge, skills, and values necessary to live out a life in which their faith life is integrated into their actions as they live out Christian values.

Reflection Questions

The following questions are posed to provide a framework for summarizing the ten components integral to a comprehensive Catholic school curriculum:

1. How does the school's philosophy reflect the Catholic nature of the school and influence the curriculum? Which gospel values are identified in the philosophy?

2. How do the curriculum decisions and activities include parents and project a positive image of the Catholic school to the public?

3. Are students assisted in gaining a balanced world view and an understanding of global interdependence? Are peace and justice concepts integrated into the curriculum and actually taught to students?

4. Is there an established procedure (perhaps recommended by the [arch]diocese) for developing curriculum policies and guidelines? Is it used by the board, principal, and faculty? What curriculum policies and/or guidelines currently exist? How are they evaluated?

5. Do the instructional strategies used in the school reflect learning theories that are in harmony with the Catholic philosophy of the school?

6. How are teachers and the school staff assisted in understanding their role in imparting gospel values in a Catholic school? Are faculty and staff involved in planning and assessing the curriculum and instructional strategies?

7. How does the content of the curriculum consider the needs and expectations of the learner, society, and the Church? How does the scope and sequence reflect gospel values?

8. Do the instructional materials reflect the school's philosophy, gospel values, and individual student's learning style?

9. Is there an organized plan for assessing curriculum? Is this cycle in harmony with curriculum planning in the (arch)diocese?

10. How is the curriculum assessed in light of the mission of the school? Does the assessment include a review of the philosophy, the scope and sequences for each content area, the instructional strategies, parent involvement in curriculum planning, the instructional materials and, how the curriculum is evaluated?

Resources

Abbott, W. M., ed. 1966. *Declaration on Christian education (Gravissimum educationis)*. In *The documents of Vatican II*, trans. Joseph Gallagher, 637–51. New York: Guild Press.

Congregation for Catholic Education. 1977. *The Catholic school*. Washington, D.C.: United States Catholic Conference.

———. 1982. *Lay Catholics in schools: Witnesses to faith*. Boston: Daughters of Saint Paul.

———. 1988. *The religious dimension of education in a Catholic school: Guidelines for reflection and renewal*. Washington, D.C.: United States Catholic Conference.

Hanlon, J. M. 1973. *Theory, practice and education*. Fond du Lac, Wis.: Marian College Press.

John Paul II. 1987. The Catholic school of the '80s. *Origins* 17(17).

National Conference of Catholic Bishops. 1972. *To teach as Jesus did: A pastoral message on Catholic education*. Washington, D.C.: United States Catholic Conference.

———. 1979. *Sharing the light of faith: National catechetical directory for Catholics of the United States*. Washington, D.C.: United States Catholic Conference.

Pius XI. 1929. *On the Christian education of youth*. Boston: Daughters of St. Paul.

The author, Sr. Donna Innes, CSA, Ph.D., is professor of Graduate Education at Marion College in Fond du Lac, Wisconsin.

The Principal as
MANAGERIAL
LEADER
◆◆◆

O verview

Managerial leadership in Catholic schools provides the "hands" or practical support wherein both spiritual and educational leadership can meaningfully and efficiently function. Reflecting on the essence of effective Catholic school management Hind states,

> Christ was the most effective executive in the history of the human race. The results He achieved are second to none. In three years, He defined a mission and formed the strategies and plans to carry it out. With a staff of twelve unlikely men, He organized Christianity. . . . He recruited, trained, and motivated twelve ordinary men to become extraordinary. He is the greatest manager and developer of people ever (1989, pp. 13–14).

The people who work in Catholic schools are the school's greatest asset. Successful Catholic school principals appreciate the loyalty and dedication of school personnel. The autonomous governance structure of Catholic schools calls for the management skills of creative problem solving and independent decision making at the school level on personnel, budgeting, and purchasing issues. Thus major areas of concern and responsibility in managerial leadership include administering human resources, nurturing institutional relationships, and facilitating the school's financial stability.

PERSONNEL MANAGEMENT

Development of people is one of the most challenging aspects of being the principal of a Catholic school. A measure of true success lies in the principal's ability to see and enhance the gifts in others, and to provide opportunities for others' gifts to benefit the school program.

The administrator must have specific skills to recruit, assess, develop, and evaluate a wide variety of personnel who fill increasingly technical positions in the modern Catholic school. Catholic school leaders also must be knowledgeable in group dynamics, budgeting, canon and civil law, public relations, governance, current technology, and long-range/strategic planning.

The following beliefs espoused by participants of the National Congress: Catholic Schools for the 21st Century (*National Congress: Catholic Schools for the 21st Century: Executive Summary* 1992) indicate the high standard expected of Catholic school leaders in their work with personnel:

- The Catholic school creates a supportive and challenging climate which affirms the dignity of all persons within the school community (p. 17).

- The recruitment, selection, and formation of leaders (and teachers) is essential to the future of Catholic schools (p. 29).

In their chapter, *The Principal's Role in Personnel Management* (page 74), Gilroy and Leak provide pertinent insights into the recruitment, selection, and development of Catholic school personnel. They remind administrators of the importance of working to establish a learning culture in the school so that each staff member finds sustained personal satisfaction, challenge, support, and continued professional renewal.

INSTITUTIONAL MANAGEMENT

Catholic school tradition is a result of "both an active engagement with the world and, at times, strong reaction to it" (Bryk, Lee, and Holland 1993, p. 15). Catholic schools were among the first institutions founded by Catholics in the New World. The foundation of these institutions stands as a glorious achievement, a monument to the hard work, support, and dedication of countless men and women.

Historically, the Catholic school in the United States has been more a systematic way of schooling rather than a tightly knit school system. As a result, schools were established and continue to be sponsored in several ways. Before 1960 Catholic schools were generally sponsored by a parish, a religious congregation, or the diocese. Since 1960 other types of Catholic schools have evolved. Inter-parish and regional schools have been formed which may be sponsored by two or more parishes or directly by the diocese. Other schools, established by independent lay boards, have sought affiliation with the Catholic Church.

Regardless of sponsorship, each school is an institution that interacts with other institutions and agencies as it goes about its business of providing educational experiences within an integral religious perspective. Institutional management encompasses skills involving a knowledge and understanding of relationships within the school and between the school and other groups. Providing a safe environment within the school promotes the effectiveness of the school program. Understanding the intricacies of the school governance structure, school law, and canon law—along with recognizing the importance of the relationship of the school to a number of groups including the local Catholic school board, the diocesan office, the religious congregation, and the local public school districts—enhances the purposes and work of the school. Being alert to the opportunities afforded by participation in federally-funded education programs might help to return to parents a portion of their tax dollars. Administering the school through the use of technology and integrating technology into the curriculum demonstrate an awareness of this potential to bring the school into the twenty-first century.

Directional statements and beliefs adopted by participants of the National Congress: Catholic Schools for the 21st Century (*National Congress* 1992) reinforce the concept of the school as an institution:

🙠 Catholic schools are an integral part of education in the United States and a valuable asset to the nation (p. 21).

🙠 Effective Catholic school governance requires the preparation, empowerment, and collaboration of the community it serves (p. 25).

🙠 Governance with the full participation of the laity is the key to the future of Catholic schools (p. 25).

The importance of fostering constructive relationships with agencies that affect the working of the school is a theme expressed by Sheehan in *The Catholic School Principal's Role: Church Governance and Structures* (page 88). She clearly differentiates the different governance structures of parish, inter-parish, diocesan, and private schools. She touches on issues such as accountability, finance, hiring, and evaluation in these governance models.

FINANCE AND DEVELOPMENT

Bryk et al. (1984) specify four issues that must be addressed to secure the future of the schools: 1) declining subsidies from the contributed services of religious personnel, 2) increasing physical plant cost due to a long history of

---

deferred maintenance, 3) the need for substantial improvement in the very low faculty salaries, and 4) the likely need to increase expenditures in response to a nationwide concern about improving the quality of schools (p. 83).

Catholic school leaders who are convinced of the need for and dedicated to the mission of Catholic schools will be cognizant of the principal's pivotal role in garnering financial support for them. Catholic schools, along with all educational institutions, are feeling the pinch of inflation and loss of revenues. The traditional means of supporting the schools have been tuition, subsidy from parishes or religious communities, and fundraising. As the ability of parishes to subsidize the financial needs of the school declines, the principal is expected to assume more responsibility and accountability for the budget and often for securing additional sources of funding to keep the schools open.

Development programs, long-range planning, marketing, and public relations programs are becoming essential to maintain the financial viability of Catholic schools. Thus Catholic school leaders face the challenge of mastering a multitude of managerial skills that have become increasingly complex and sophisticated in the last twenty-five years.

The financial management of the school affects students and their families. It impacts every employee and all aspects of the school's educational program. Even with the best of intentions, the comprehensive educational program will be in precarious circumstances without an adequate financial foundation.

Directional statements and beliefs adopted by participants of the National Congress: Catholic Schools for the 21st Century (*National Congress* 1992) present a financial vision and agenda for those in Catholic school leadership:

❧ Beliefs (p. 25):

- ❦ The financial future of Catholic schools demands securing new and available resources.
- ❦ Catholic schools are essential to the life and future of the Church in the United States and require the support of the entire Catholic community.
- ❦ Catholic schools should be available and financially accessible to Catholic families and to others who support the mission.

🖎 Directional Statements (p. 26):

- 🐦 We will challenge the entire Catholic community and others to make a radical commitment to Catholic schools and generous investment in them.
- 🐦 We will immediately initiate long-range strategic planning processes for Catholic schools at the local, diocesan and national levels.
- 🐦 We will implement in every school just compensation plans for all Catholic school personnel.
- 🐦 We will implement and evaluate comprehensive development programs at the local, diocesan, and national levels.

Konzen presents a systematic account of the issues involved in assuring the financial viability of the school in *The Prinipal's Role in Finance and Development* (page 97). His premise is that careful financial management and fostering development opportunities are critical to the continuation of the school's religious and academic mission.

The Principal's Role in Personnel Management

(Ann) Nancy Gilroy and Lawrence E. Leak, Ph.D.

> *We demand that innovation, experimentation,*
> *risk taking, collaboration, and collegiality*
> *be the hallmark of Catholic school leadership.*
>
> —*National Congress:*
> *Catholic Schools for the 21st Century:*
> *Exectuive Summary*, 1992, p. 30.

Introduction

The Catholic school is an important and significant institution in our society. It is a functional community (Coleman and Hoffer 1987) where youthful, inexperienced minds are exposed to the intellectual discipline and moral values, rooted in the Christian heritage, which will serve the individual throughout life. Not only society as a whole, but also the life of each individual is influenced by the quality of schools embodied in the quality of teaching and the quality of instruction. While the learner, as the primary beneficiary, seriously affects schooling outcomes, the critical component in determining the quality of the school lies with the leadership of the principal (Sergiovanni 1987).

Schein (1992) contends that an important role for leaders is developing "a learning organization" that is capable of perpetual diagnosis leading to higher levels of excellence. Prudent personnel management practices enable Catholic school principals to exercise considerable responsibility for establishing a collegial learning culture among the school's instructional team.

In learning organizations, a value-based mission guides action and governs the behavior of its members. Values serve to shape and reinforce a constancy of purpose and shared learning culture (Schein 1992). Because Catholic schools are faith-filled, value-based communities, they provide ideal environments for the formulation of learning organizations.

By working together principals and teachers establish a learning culture in which each staff member finds sustained personal satisfaction, challenge, support, and continued professional renewal. Thus the importance of the principal's role with respect to personnel management is based upon three basic assumptions:

- ❧ Education takes place in individual Catholic schools through dedicated school personnel who offer educational experiences that are consistent with the unique mission of the Catholic schools.
- ❧ Personal enrichment, professional development, and Christian formation are lifelong quests requiring sustained personal and organizational commitment.
- ❧ There is no substitute for the teacher who models the Christian message.

In carrying out the mission of the Catholic school, the principal leads the community—students, teachers, and parents—toward the formation of values consistent with the Catholic tradition and improved educational outcomes. The requirements of personnel management are often unrelenting, demanding enormous amounts of energy and time. Prudent attention to these issues is an important part of the principal's leadership efforts. Principals will accomplish little without the cooperation and dedication of others. The success of the school relies on the competent and committed performance of many people. When principals selectively recruit teachers and carefully facilitate their growth, they empower the effective functioning of the school (Sergiovanni 1987) as both an educational institution and a Christian community.

Personnel search and selection

Within any learning organization culture, one of the most important responsibilities of the leader is securing new personnel who are capable and willing to support the mission of the institution. Convey (1992) notes that finding the "right fit" in choosing Catholic school personnel will affect the teacher's satisfaction, success, and longevity as well as student achievement. Therefore, the selection of instructional personnel is a crucial function of the Catholic school leader.

The selection process begins with the recruitment of candidates. Deliberate attention should be given to extending this invitation to a cross-section of individuals reflective of the multicultural perspective of the Catholic Church (*National Congress* 1992). This is particularly critical in schools that boast of a culturally and ethnically diverse population. In some dioceses, recruitment is managed through central services with a list of possible candidates forwarded to the local administrator. When no such service is available, the principal will often advertise the position. Although word of mouth and local church bulletins are cost-effective means of circulating news of the opening, more formal searching through the local colleges and universities might be more fruitful.

No attempt to provide guidance in evaluating the candidate's academic preparedness or intellectual competency is made here. Those dimensions can be ascertained through careful scrutiny of transcripts and letters of recommendation. The more difficult qualities to ascertain in the interview process are those somewhat illusive traits that identify an individual's capacity to perform appropriately for teaching in the unique environment of the Catholic school.

There are many people who are committed to teaching; however, only a small percentage of them are equipped and dedicated to teaching in a Catholic school. Convey (1992, p. 111) summarizes three special qualifications for Catholic school teachers. Catholic school teachers must be

- witnesses to the faith (*Lay Catholics in Schools: Witness to Faith* 1982, no. 29), by being committed to helping students develop Christian beliefs and values;
- willing to model for their students "how these beliefs and values shape and inform spiritual, moral, and lifestyle choices" (Benson and Guerra 1985, p. 2);
- alert for opportunities to initiate the appropriate dialogue between faith and culture (*Lay Catholics in Schools: Witness to Faith* 1982, no. 29).

Regardless of religious affiliation, this mission orientation makes an important difference in the work-satisfaction of the teacher in a Catholic school where work conditions and expectations are different from those encountered in other school systems (Ciriello 1988). During the recruitment phase principals who include "mission-orientated incentives" (Tarr, Ciriello, and Convey 1993) widen their chances of attracting candidates who will value the unique opportunities offered in the Catholic school environment. The opportunities to build community with peers and students and to experience faith experiences such as shared prayer are two mission-orientated incentives that will appeal to some applicants. The degree to which an applicant is motivated by a desire to be in an environment that is compatible with personal values (Ciriello 1988) and committed to teaching in a Catholic school is significant to future performance and should be assessed during the interview (SRI Gallup 1991).

Research conducted through SRI Gallup (1991) identified ten themes that characterize the effective Catholic school teacher:

- **Dedication:** committed to teaching and to Catholic education
- **Achiever:** driven to make things happen, to make students feel "smart"
- **Relator:** causes students to want to learn and to be receptive to Catholic values
- **Developer:** motivates students to go beyond themselves
- **Empathy:** aware of the students' feelings; helping students feel their ideas matter
- **Student Rapport:** enjoys youngsters, has an interest in students' lives
- **Stimulator:** has an intensely active style which results in a "positive hum" among students
- **Faith:** integrates one's career choice with strong religious beliefs
- **Concept:** knows what is important for students and plans how to achieve it in the classroom
- **Responsibility:** views teaching as total commitment which may entail going beyond "the call of duty"

These themes call for a number of qualities to be discerned in the interview:

Listening and **observation** are critical qualities of the Catholic school teacher in order to perceive the student as an individual with a unique learning style and pace (SRI Gallup 1991). What strategies has the applicant for learning about the students individually? How will the applicant seek to learn the uniqueness of each child?

Positive morale in the classroom is critical to the learning environment (SRI Gallup 1991). How will the teacher promote an atmosphere of camaraderie and compassion in the classroom? How will each child be encouraged to see him/herself as a special child of God and valuable member of the class?

Motivating students toward self-actualization and having high expectations of all students is critical to students' success (SRI Gallup 1991). Does the applicant indicate the importance of ensuring each child's progress? What measures will the teacher take to encourage the individual gifts of each child?

A sense of **humor** is an important way to activate children. Does the applicant display a sense of humor or a playful spirit? Does the applicant understand the place of humor as a way to encourage learning?

The **time** commitment required of any teacher is significantly more than the average eight-hour day. The Catholic school teacher must attend to the whole child in its spiritual as well intellectual development. This responsibility may require the teacher to spend additional time on collateral activities in addition to regular teaching responsibilities. What indications does the applicant give of a willingness to participate in all aspects of the school program?

Efficient **planning** and **organization** are critical for Catholic school teachers in order to bring out the best in the students (SRI Gallup 1991). How does the teacher go about instructional planning? What evidence does the teacher give that the focus of planning and organization should emphasize the welfare of the students rather than the smooth running of the classroom?

It is important to underscore the significance of determining the individual's strong **faith orientation** during the selection process. This quality identifies a great deal about the internal motivation of the applicant for the position. The teacher with a strong faith theme will promote the spiritual growth of the student, the primary function of the Catholic school (SRI Gallup 1991). Ideally, the teacher who demonstrates an understanding of the catechetical documents and dogma of the Catholic Church will be well fortified to integrate gospel values into daily lessons. However, some promising candidates may lack this formal knowledge. It will be the responsibility of the principal to supply experiences and resources to compensate for this lack.

Finally, although it is sometimes awkward to discuss something as personal as one's prayer life, it is important that the principal during the search process ensure that the prospective teacher has an ongoing sense of the sacred in his/her life. The candidate should understand the additional responsibility associated with being a Catholic school teacher. "It is important to explore with applicants their personal values and orientation toward the mission . . ." (Tarr, Ciriello, and Convey 1993). As the person in most direct contact with the student, the teacher must model an exemplary **Christian life style** and be prepared to share his/her values with young people.

Staff development

Hiring is just the first step toward developing an effective faculty. Ongoing formation is critical if the teacher is to catch "glimpses of God" in his/her work (Droel 1989). Since teachers are constantly called upon to "give" in the course of their day, it is important that they be able to "receive" to sustain their sense of ministry. Programs for personal growth, professional growth, and religious growth create opportunities for replenishment of spirit and result in higher levels of teacher commitment (Tarr, Ciriello, and Convey 1993). The effective principal provides, throughout the year, various opportunities for the teachers to be stimulated, motivated, and enriched. McBride (1981) provides an excellent resource for designing Christian formation programs. In all cases, such programs ought to be empowering, developed through consensus, and respectful of adult learning principles.

As the principal values the teachers and fosters an environment of mutual trust, the teachers will reciprocate with loyalty (Covey 1991). The effective principal creates a culture in which teachers feel a sense of empowerment in carrying out the mission of the Catholic school. This is important because organizations that empower enable the individual to feel competent (Bennis 1985). Teachers begin to feel a part of something larger than themselves and begin to identify with the institution.

The effective leader employs a consensus form of decision making in the process of developing a personnel development program (Covey 1991). The staff, those who are most impacted by these programs, work with the administrator in planning such programs and in formulating goals and objectives to achieve the overarching vision and mission.

The principal's efforts will be fruitful when appeals to the teacher tap the intrinsic reward system out of which the teacher operates (Sergiovanni 1992). Adult learners bring their best effort to a task when their interest is piqued and they feel that they are able to make a significant contribution to an endeavor. Sergiovanni claims that the common mentality of "what gets rewarded, gets done" discourages people from becoming self-managed and self-motivated. Such a reward system is not primary to Catholic school teachers who are challenged by the call of the ministry to serve and who find satisfaction in their labors.

Personnel appraisal for ongoing professional renewal

Personnel appraisal and professional renewal are central to improving schools. Since we are dynamic creatures, ever in the process of renewal, rarely arriving at fixed points, periodic appraisal enables us to assess where we are in order to move toward perfecting our professional and personal practice. Catholic school principals use appraisal to support teachers professionally. Principals can significantly influence teachers' performance and career path with systematic appraisal combined with systematic professional staff development activities (Joyce and Showers 1995).

While considering the variety of existing models of personnel appraisal and professional renewal systems, it is important to respect the tenant that teachers' commitment to personnel appraisal is directly related to their involvement in all aspects of the system or process. Castetter (1986) suggests six general stages in a systematic assessment and renewal program that includes teacher involvement:

First, Catholic school principals must capture the essence of a teacher's responsibilities. These responsibilities form the basis for developing the appraisal process. Many of these responsibilities formed the basis of the hiring interview and should be quite familiar to the teacher. The responsibilities appropriately reflect the unique faith environment of the school and will include objective as well as subjective information concerning the teacher's involvement in the community and spiritual life of the school. The task-related responsibilities are qualities that can be observed and measured by those assigned to conduct performance appraisals.

Second, school principals and teachers create the performance goals together. Teachers must be given a great deal of input toward the formulation of performance goals because they hold the key to goal attainment. Obviously, these goals should be clear, realistic, within the teacher's power to control, linked to the mission of the school, and project a desired end result. By working with teachers to establish goals, principals can: 1) clarify work-related behavior, 2) communicate performance expectations, 3) emphasize delegating and empowerment strategies, 4) establish a foundation for personnel appraisal and professional renewal, and 5) articulate the teacher's role in carrying out the mission.

Third, information is gathered with appropriate care respecting the moral and legal implications for personnel appraisal processes. Gathering information requires thoughtful attention to teacher behavior. Catholic school principals should be mindful of the multiple sources of objective data readily available for assessing teacher performance.

Fourth, the performance of teachers is assessed. The principal and teacher dialogue about task-related activities that lead to goal attainment. A number of issues can cause the assessment of teacher performance to become quite complex. Issues such as task difficulty, task interdependence, and uncontrollable circumstances are multiple contributors to performance goals. For principals, attempting to balance individual fairness with organizational consistency can prove to be a constant personnel management challenge. As we have noted, there are many non-task dimensions to the Catholic teacher's role which must also be assessed. This requires both sensitivity and candor from the principal. If such feedback is not provided, the role of the Catholic school teacher is functionary and not, therefore, supportive of the Catholic school culture.

Fifth, there is communication of assessment findings. This step is probably the most intensive step of the process and one that requires the greatest amount

---

of sensitivity from Catholic school principals. Moreover, it is most important to remember that this step is also an information-gathering point of the appraisal and renewal process where clarifying data from both parties are shared and considered. Teachers need to feel invited to respond to the principal's analysis and dialogue about any discrepancies which may emerge. Care must be given to bring closure to those matters.

Sixth, professional renewal, the final step of the process, is a continuous activity involving personal planning, action, and energy. Individualized professional renewal plans build upon the job-related strengths of the individual teachers and seek to enhance their knowledge, skills, and abilities. Renewal plans consider the religious dimension of the school as integral to the formulation of personal goals and objectives. Catholic school principals who model their commitment to professional renewal by participating in developmental activities can significantly influence the professional renewal route teachers travel.

Process skills for personnel management

Catholic school principals make a difference in their schools through facilitating change and improvement by providing leadership in a faith context to teachers, students, and parents. Catholic school principals are also managers as they maintain the stability and security of a school organization. Both dimensions of leadership (change) and management (stability) result in the role of the principalship being a dynamic opportunity and responsibility calling for a continuous interplay between change and stability.

Since the personnel are the heart and soul of any institution, the principal relies on "people skills" to nudge the school organization to increasing levels of effectiveness. Among the many skills deserving the attention of Catholic school principals, group process and team building skills, along with delegation and empowerment skills, are often cited as the most essential for effective personnel management. In addition conflict management skills are essential to any effective administrator.

Group process and team-building skills. Work-related activity done in school environments organized around groups or teams which foster social and professional interaction is essential for institutionalizing change in schools (Sergiovanni 1987). Educationally, just as students are grouped for instruction, so too, organizing teachers by grade-level groups or teams is an effective way to accomplish educational objectives. Research indicates that one of the impediments to school improvement is teacher isolation (Sergiovanni 1987). Enhancing the group process and team-building skills of Catholic school principals and teachers for purposes of improving personnel relations and creating superior standards of academic excellence enhances morale and encourages creativity (Cunningham and Gresso 1994) and supports school improvement (Sergiovanni 1987).

Team building is an effective strategy for bringing school personnel together around a common mission. Productive utilization of group process and team building allows teachers and administrators to interact in ways that are innovative and creative. Scholtes (1988) states that successful teams have several common characteristics: 1) clarity in team goals, 2) an improvement plan linked to an organizational mission, 3) clearly defined team member roles, 4) clear communication processes, 5) beneficial team member behavior, 6) ground rules and decision-making procedures, and 7) significant contributions by all team members.

Among the beneficial aspects of team building is creating an environment where teachers are empowered to build lasting solutions to complex problems (Maeroff 1993). Catholic school teachers, who view themselves as knowledgeable sources of imaginative solutions, generate an amazing pool of creative energy. In addition, Catholic school principals who develop, nurture, and sustain a culture that taps the knowledge, expertise, and spiritual energy of teachers are practicing collegiality which is a fundamental principle of collaboration espoused by the Catholic Church (Reid 1990).

Delegation and empowerment skills. "Give a man a fish and you feed him for a day. Teach a man to fish and you feed him for a lifetime." This Chinese proverb captures the essence of delegation and empowerment. As Catholic school principals work to build productive teams of teachers, they set the stage for teachers to assume more responsibility. Secretan (1993) believes "the highest-quality decisions are made in organizations where power is diffused and responsibility is moved to the lowest appropriate levels" (p. 229). This concept is the definition of the principle of subsidiarity first espoused in Catholic circles by Pope Pius XI (Reid 1990) and since reaffirmed in the documents of the Second Vatican Council. Catholic school leaders who employ collegiality and subsidiarity not only employ reliable management skills but also model two important principles that are basic to Catholic culture.

In a nurturing environment, Catholic school teachers, as competent professionals, are capable and willing to make high-quality decisions about ways to maintain excellence. Through delegation and empowerment, principals convey the values of trust and professional respect to personnel who have chosen to be members of a faith community. Secretan (1993) contends that delegation "is a statement of respect and love for others." But he cautions that "delegation can be successful only when the delegator has a caring eye and a teaching heart" (p. 248). Delegation and empowerment drive the motivational desires of professionals (Secretan 1993). Catholic school principals motivate their teaching personnel by enabling individuals to exercise their unique gifts and through the power of total staff involvement.

To delegate effectively, Catholic school principals should be mindful of the following points:

- match assignments with the knowledge, skills, and abilities of the individuals or teams;
- delegate gradually as confidence and competence of individuals build;
- delegate the whole assignment and avoid attempts to micro-manage individuals or teams;
- communicate and negotiate for specific assignment outcome;
- delegate task-related, decision-making, and problem-solving authority to individuals/team members;
- express positive expectations for success.

Conflict management. It is a fact of life that, even in the most satisfying environment, conflicts will emerge between and among people. To foster a constructive environment the principal seeks not only to create conditions that minimize conflicts, but also to facilitate the resolution of conflicts as they emerge (SRI Gallup 1990).

Always mindful of the fact that the Catholic school is a faith community which values the individual and which respects the diversity among people, the principal has a variety of tactics to use in conflict management. The effective principal manages the inevitable conflicts that arise by taking into consideration the needs of the individuals involved. The administrator listens carefully and gives priority to the concerns of the individual teacher (SRI Gallup 1990). Seeking the common ground upon which the different members of the school community meet is a way of managing conflict.

In some cases administrators believe that the greatest attention ought to be given to those tasks that enable the job to be accomplished. But when task accomplishment is stressed at the expense of consideration of the persons involved, hurt feelings and low morale may result (Hersey and Blanchard 1984). Catholic school teachers respond more positively when they perceive that they are working *with* the principal rather than *for* the principal (Ciriello 1988). Conflict is minimized and tasks effectively completed when individuals are treated as professionals (Sergiovanni 1992).

The words of Abraham in Genesis: "Let there be no strife between you and me . . . for we are kinsmen," (Gn 13:8) serves well as a model of harmony to motivate the Catholic school principal and teacher to find peaceful resolutions to conflict so that ultimately the student will experience true community.

Conclusion and reflection

The selection of Catholic school teachers must consider the unique culture of the Catholic school, a culture which will be shaped by the very process of selection. Training is available to assist principals in this critical task (cf: SRI Gallup 1990).

Recent studies indicate that Catholic school teachers have high levels of satisfaction in their ministry (Tarr, Ciriello, and Convey 1993). Many factors contribute to this: collegial processes, involvement in shaping the future of the school, high degree of autonomy in the classroom, good relationship with administration. This experience of job satisfaction results in commitment and dedication which are the hallmark of Catholic schools. The principal creates the climate in which this is made possible.

Contemporary school leaders shape a culture in which moral commitment between principal and teacher becomes a norm. Catholic schools, a significant part of the Church's educative ministry, are institutions built on a strong foundation of faith. Within these schools are educators who desire to make contributions that enhance the intellectual and spiritual development of students. Catholic school principals transform their schools into innovative learning organizations by valuing and developing their staffs.

Reflection Questions

1. Considering your personal leadership style, to what extent will you encourage the instructional staff to be involved in shaping the vision and carrying out the mission of the school? What are the advantages and disadvantages of your perspective?

2. Give specific examples of ways to motivate teachers extrinsically and intrinsically?

3. What aspects of group dynamics enhance consensus decision making?

4. What is the responsibility of the administrator when conflicts arise between the administrator and teacher?

5. How would you describe the "learning culture" of a specific school with which you are familiar?

6. What are specific ways a principal can demonstrate sensitivity to the uniqueness of the individual teacher?

7. How can the principal provide for the ongoing Christian formation of the teacher?

8. What significant questions in an interview will elicit information about the prospective teacher's behavior in various situations?

9. What are activities that provide continuous professional development for school personnel?

10. What kind of information might be included on an appraisal form for a new teacher and a continuing teacher?

11. What efforts can be made to select and sustain a culturally diverse staff?

12. What specific interview questions would provide information about a teacher's prayer life, value-orientation, and mission-orientation?

Resources

Bennis, W. 1985. *Leaders.* New York: Harper and Row.

Benson, P. L., and M. J. Guerra. 1985. *Sharing the faith: The beliefs and values of Catholic high school teachers.* Washington, D.C.: National Catholic Educational Association.

Castetter, W. B. 1986. *The personnel function in educational administration.* 4th ed. New York: MacMillan.

Ciriello, M. J. 1988. Teachers in Catholic school: A study of commitment. Ph.D. diss., The Catholic University of America, 1987. Abstract in *Dissertations Abstracts International* 48:8514A.

Ciriello, M. J., and J. J. Convey. 1993. Catholic higher education and diocesan school departments collaborating to strengthen leadership. *Current Issues in Catholic Higher Education* 14(1):34–39.

Clifton, D., and P. Nelson. 1992. *Soar with your strengths.* New York: Delacourte Press.

Coleman, J. S., and T. Hoffer. 1987. *Public and private high schools: The impact of communities.* New York: Basic Books.

Congregation for Catholic Education. 1977. *The Catholic school.* Washington, D.C.: United States Catholic Conference.

———. 1982. *Lay Catholics in schools: Witnesses to faith.* Boston: Daughters of St. Paul.

Convey, J. J. 1992. *Catholic schools make a difference.* Washington, D.C.: National Catholic Educational Association.

Covey, S. R. 1991. *Principle-centered leadership.* New York: Simon and Schuster.

Cunningham, W. G., and D. W. Gresso. 1994. *Cultural leadership: The culture of excellence in education.* Needham, Mass.: Allyn and Bacon.

Droel, W. 1989. *The spirituality of work: Teachers.* Chicago: National Center for the Laity.

Hersey, P., and K. H. Blanchard. 1984. *The management of organizational behavior,* 4th ed. Englewood Cliffs, N.J.: Prentice-Hall.

Joyce, B., and B. Showers. 1995. Student achievement through staff development: Fundamentals of school renewal. White Plains, N.Y.: Longman.

Larson, C. E., and F. M. LaFasto. 1991. *Teamwork.* Newbury Park, Calif.: Sage Publications.

Leak, L., B. McKay, P. Splain, P. Walker, and C. Held. 1990. *Professional development resource book for school principals.* College Park, Md.: University of Maryland Printing Service.

Maeroff, G. I. 1993. Team building. *Phi Delta Kappan* 74 (7):512–19.

McBride, A. A. 1981. *The Christian formation of Catholic educators, A CACE monograph.* Washington, D.C.: National Catholic Educational Association.

National Catholic Educational Association. 1982. *Code of ethics for the Catholic school teacher.* Washington, D.C.

National Conference of Catholic Bishops. 1990. *In support of Catholic elementary and secondary schools.* Washington, D.C.: United States Catholic Conference.

National Congress: Catholic Schools for the 21st Century. 1992. *Leadership of and on behalf of Catholic schools.* In *National congress: Catholic schools for the 21st century: Executive summary*, eds. M. Guerra, R. Haney, and R. Kealey. Washington, D.C.: National Catholic Educational Association.

Reid, D. G., ed. 1990. *Dictionary of Christianity in America.* Downers Grove, Ill.: Intervarsity Press.

Schein, E. 1992. *Organizational culture and leadership.* 2d ed. San Francisco: Jossey-Bass Publishers.

Scholtes, P. 1989. *The team handbook.* Madison, Wis.: Joiner Associates.

Secretan, L. H. K. 1993. *Managerial moxie.* Rocklin, Calif.: Prima Publishing.

Sergiovanni, T. J. 1987. *The principalship: A reflective practice perspective.* Boston: Allyn and Bacon.

———. 1992. *Moral leadership: Getting to the heart of school improvement.* San Francisco: Jossey-Bass Publishers.

SRI Gallup. 1990. Themes of the Catholic school principal. In *The Catholic school principal perceiver: Concurrent validity report.* Lincoln, Neb.: Human Resources for Ministry Institute.

———. 1991. Themes of the Catholic school teacher. In *The Catholic school principal perceiver: Concurrent validity report.* Lincoln, Neb.: Human Resources for Ministry Institute.

Tarr, H. C. 1990a. *Teacher values and commitment orientations.* A Report to the Archdiocese of Boston Strategic Planning Study for Schools, October 29, 1990. Washington, D.C.: The Catholic University of America.

———. 1990b. *Teacher satisfaction, attitudes and attributions.* A Report for the Archdiocese of Boston Strategic Planning Study for Schools, December 21, 1990. Washington, D.C.: The Catholic University of America.

Tarr H. C., M. J. Ciriello, and J. J. Convey. 1993. Commitment and satisfaction among parochial school teachers: Findings from Catholic education. *Journal of Research on Christian Education* 2(1):41–63.

The authors, (Ann) Nancy Gilroy and Lawrence E. Leak, Ph.D., are assistant superintendent in the Archdiocese of Baltimore and associate professor at Morgan State University in Baltimore, Maryland, respectively.

The Catholic School Principal's Role: Church Governance and Structures

Lourdes Sheehan, RSM

Introduction

Because Catholic schools are an integral part of the Church's mission, it is essential for the principal to understand how the school relates to the parish(es), diocese, and/or religious congregation that sponsor it. Each of the four types of Catholic schools—parish, interparish (also called regional or consolidated), diocesan, and private—has differing funding sources and governance structures within which it operates. There is no one set of policies, much less practices, that operates in all Catholic schools. In spite of its image as a hierarchical organization with universally enforced norms, the Church's policies and practices of educational governance and accountability are neither uniformly defined nor universally practiced in Catholic schools.

There is a great deal of local autonomy at both the diocesan and parish levels so that what really happens in a school depends on local personalities, policies, and politics. The information and suggestions which follow are based on commonly understood principles and church law. It is essential for the principal to be well-informed about the diocese's and/or religious community's educational policies and to apply these general comments to her/his specific situation.

Definitions

A *parish school* is defined as an institution (elementary or secondary) that is associated with only one parish. This parish community provides spiritual, communal, and financial support (sometimes called subsidy).

Those schools that serve and are supported by more than one parish are called *interparish*, *regional*, or *consolidated* schools. The terms "interparish" and "regional" are often used interchangeably, but use of the term "consolidated" is usually reserved to describe the merger of two or more existing schools that may be located at more than one site. In practice, however, the responsibilities of the principal are the same. Usually the financial support flows directly from the parishes to the school, and all parishes share responsibility for spiritual and communal support.

A *diocesan school* is one that is not identified with any one parish or group of parishes and ordinarily the subsidy goes directly from the diocese to the school. Principals of diocesan schools need to ensure spiritual and communal support from those parishes that send students to the school.

Traditionally, *private schools* are those that are owned, operated, and sponsored by a religious congregation that is responsible for the school's support. Recently, some religious congregations have established boards of trustees and charged them with the responsibility for operating the schools. In these instances, usually the congregation maintains a sponsorship relationship with the institution. Some private schools have been started by lay boards of trustees which must work out the school's formal relationship with the diocesan bishop in order to call the school Catholic.

Parish schools

Approximately 74 percent of the Catholic elementary (6,052) and secondary (141) schools in the United States are operated as a single parish school (Brigham 1993). Ultimately, each is the responsibility of the pastor of the parish who according to church law is the canonical administrator of the entire parish including the school. Ordinarily, the pastor is assisted by the active participation of parishioners on a finance council (*Code of Canon Law* Book V, Title II), pastoral council, and school board/committee. These collegial bodies are constituted as consultative to the pastor.

In practice, it is the school principal who functions as the actual administrator of the school. The principal is the parish staff member who works most closely with the school board/committee and/or other school parent groups. The key to the effective operation of the school and ultimately the parish is a compatible working relationship between the pastor and principal marked by frequent communication and mutual respect and trust.

Hiring Practices

When the majority of principals were appointed by the religious congregations, hiring was not the issue it is today. The question of who hires is basic to the understanding of accountability. The parish is obligated to follow diocesan policy in this and all other education matters. However, because of differing practices and the emerging role of boards, it is necessary for the

---

principal to understand hiring practices as well as roles and relationships among parish leaders.

Recognizing that the pastor has the final word and is, as a matter of fact, the "employer" of the principal, Father John Gilbert (1983), an experienced educator and pastor, believes that the pastor should make it an absolute practice that no principal is hired without the involvement and consent of both the board and the staff with whom the principal works. There are many ways to ensure this involvement. The most common is to establish a search/interview committee whose members include those individuals and groups whose relationship with the principal affects the running of the school.

While the pastor should be in close communication with this committee, it does not seem essential that he attend each and every meeting. It would be unfortunate, however, if he were never involved and simply received the final recommendations from the committee without the benefit of prior discussion. Somewhere between no involvement and running the committee there is a middle ground which will ensure agreement on the job description or role of the principal and on the specific needs of the parish and school.

Ordinarily, the principal is responsible for hiring faculty and staff. Some policies require that the diocese approve applicants for teaching positions prior to their being hired. Others state that the pastor, and sometimes the diocese, must approve all contracts before they are binding.

Evaluation Practices

Standard personnel practice recognizes that the person who hires is the one ultimately responsible for evaluation and continuation of the contract. The principal will want to ensure regular discussions with the pastor to provide a good basis for the more formal evaluation carried out at least every three years. This process usually involves those other groups with which the principal relates. Most dioceses have well-established processes and procedures for evaluation and offer the services of the education staff to assist both the principal and pastor. In those infrequent instances where a dispute arises over the principal's contract, both parties have the opportunity to appeal to the diocesan arbitration and conciliation process.

The principal is primarily responsible for regular written evaluations of faculty and staff according to diocesan policies and procedures.

Accountability Issues

The relationship of the parish school board and the principal is influenced by the way other consultative bodies are established and function in the parish. If the parish school board/committee has the understanding that it is "policy-making" and has actually hired the principal, then in a very real sense the principal is the "employee" of the board. In the more common practice, the board has been consulted in the hiring process and the pastor actually signs the contract. In any case the question of all relationships needs clarification. Regardless of the accountability structure, honest and collaborative discussion among the principal, board, and pastor is always the ideal when considering the welfare of the school.

In a very real sense, the principal is accountable to the parents who have entrusted their children to the faculty and staff of the school. While this relationship cannot, strictly speaking, be put under the category of governance, it is very real and demands that the principal possess a commitment to availability and communication with all parents. All of the effectiveness research, especially that reported in the *Effective Catholic School Study* (Bryk et al. 1984), reports that one of the most significant indicators of an effective school is that faculty, parents, and students share a common vision and commitment to the mission of the school. There is no way in which this important factor can be achieved without time and effort being spent on communication.

Interparish schools

Because the number of interparish schools, including regional and consolidated ones, is growing, the principal of such a school needs to pay special attention to questions of governance and accountability. At the present time they constitute 10 percent (855) of all Catholic schools; 9.7 percent, or 703, are elementary and 12 percent, or 152, are secondary (Brigham 1993). The challenges facing the principal of this type of school are unique.

Governance and Management

In the other three types of schools, the lines of accountability within which the principal functions are clear: in a parish school, the principal is directly accountable to the pastor; in a private school, to the major superior of the religious congregation or board of trustees; and in a diocesan school, to the bishop through the superintendent. However, because an interparish school serves equally a number of parishes, its principal is directly accountable to more than one pastor. When a school board is involved, the issue of accountability becomes more complicated.

Dioceses are establishing new types of governance structures to address these schools. Some call for the bishop to appoint, from among the supporting pastors, one who will serve as the "school pastor." In this instance, the principal relates to this pastor in a manner similar to that of a parish school principal. Other dioceses are rethinking the role of the board in an interparish school and giving it delegated authority to operate the school within diocesan guidelines. Often all of the pastors and representatives of supporting parishes are members of the board. In this latter case, the relationship of the principal and such a board differs from that of the parish school principal and board. Principals of such schools will need to meet with diocesan education staff to clarify and understand the governance structure.

Other Issues

There are two issues important to the principal which are common to all Catholic schools.

Relationship of school to diocese

The diocesan superintendent of schools has the responsibility to see that diocesan educational policies are implemented in each school. The superintendent and staff usually schedule regular meetings with principals to discuss diocesan policies and procedures and are available to visit individual schools and provide direct assistance to the principal.

New principals, in particular, should obtain and study the diocesan education manual which will provide specific information about such matters as curriculum, personnel policies, lines of accountability, and various policies which affect students, health and safety regulations, and state and federal regulations.

Local, state, and federal education programs

The individual principal may have limited contact with the local, state, and federal education agencies, but has the responsibility, nevertheless, to know applicable statutes and regulations which affect non-governmental schools (also referred to as private schools). The Department of Education of the United States Catholic Conference regularly forwards information regarding federal issues, and state Catholic conferences send material from the state to the superintendent, who in turn gives these and appropriate local information to the principals.

Diocesan schools

Diocesan schools (581) comprise 35.5 percent, or 444, of the secondary and 2 percent, or 137, of the elementary Catholic schools in this country (Brigham 1993). A principal of a diocesan school is directly accountable to the diocese. In practice, this usually means that the responsibility is to the bishop through the superintendent of schools and some type of board structure at either the school or diocesan level.

Governance and Management

Since the practice of designating elementary schools as diocesan seems to be relatively new, there is no traditional pattern to cite. However, at the secondary level the past practice in many dioceses was to have a diocesan priest serve as the principal of the school. In those instances where a woman religious or lay person was appointed principal, the usual practice was for the bishop to appoint a priest as director, coordinator, or school pastor. The intent of such a practice was to establish clear lines of accountability between the school and diocese. In many dioceses, this is no longer the practice with the result that the issue of the principal's accountability is not as clear.

Finances

Most diocesan secondary school principals relate to some type of board. In some instances, the diocesan school board is responsible to the bishop for recommending policies, especially financial ones. While individual principals are not usually members of such a board, they are often invited to make presentations and may be called in as consultants. The diocesan superintendent of schools is the educational staff person to whom the board relates. Some diocesan principals establish local advisory boards with whom they consult on local matters. More recently, such boards are assuming responsibilities in the area of development, including public relations and marketing.

Private schools

While much of what has already been noted about principals of parish schools also applies to private schools, it is important to acknowledge that those who serve as administrators of private schools have unique relationships to the religious congregations and/or boards of trustees responsible for the schools.

Schools operated by religious congregations are the largest percentage of Catholic secondary schools at 35.5 percent, or 512. At the elementary level, private schools are the smallest group at 3.5 percent, or 282 (Brigham 1993). Traditionally, Catholic private schools (794 total) have enjoyed the clearest lines of authority and accountability. For years, the principal was a member of the religious congregation and was appointed by the superior to serve a specific term. In practice, the principal enjoyed almost total autonomy in the daily administration of the school and the evaluation of personnel. When that practice changes, all parties need clarity and understanding regarding roles and relationships.

Governance and Management

As more religious congregations establish boards that include non-congregational members, the issues of governance and management need clarification. More often than not, the key point of discussion is the hiring of the principal and, therefore, the relation of that person to the religious congregation and to the board. When the administrator is a member of the congregation, that issue is not as complicated as it is when a lay person assumes that position. As fewer religious assume such roles, a person considering working as principal in a private school needs to understand existing relationships and expectations of both the congregation and board. Often the congregation will appoint one of its members to work with the lay principal and board during such a transition.

Finances

Most private schools operate without significant financial support from either the diocese or the religious congregation. The board usually has the responsibility for operating the school with a balanced budget. The principal is charged with operating the school within that approved amount.

Principals of private schools should be aware that the relationship between some congregations and their board are in the development stage. Therefore there may be some unresolved issues. An example of such an issue is who has responsibility for capital improvements and repairs to the school facilities. One approach may be for the congregation to recognize its role as "landlord" and function in this manner with regard to major repairs and renovations. This model assumes that the board of trustees will function as a "tenant" and may allocate a percentage of the operating budget as either rent or contingency for upkeep. Since the principal will be ultimately responsible for the administration of the budget, it is important that he/she has a solid understanding of all related issues.

Relationship with the Diocese

Traditionally, private schools have operated in dioceses as a significant part of the congregation's mission. The bishop has ordinarily related to the school through the major superior of the congregation. Most private schools cooperate with the diocesan schools office and are subject to follow diocesan policies in the areas of religious education. This recognizes the authority of the bishop as the chief catechist.

When private schools are not directly related with a religious congregation, both the principal and board need to be clear about how the formal relationship with the bishop is both established and maintained.

Conclusion and reflection

In order to function effectively, the local Catholic school principal needs to know how the Catholic Church is organized.

The general descriptions of how the four major types of schools are organized and function will help potential and new principals understand terminology and, perhaps, ask the right questions.

The principal should remember what was said earlier in this article about what really influences the governance and accountability of Catholic schools—personalities, politics, and policies present at the local level. This is the real situation; however, this comment need not be construed in a negative manner. It remains true that local autonomy is one of the best-kept secrets in Catholic schools, and, I believe, contributes to the school's effectiveness. The effective principal will observe the local scene and determine in consultation with a mentor and the diocesan education staff how to function most effectively.

The challenges facing the Catholic school principal in the areas of governance and structure should be seen as neither overwhelming nor insurmountable. The most effective principal will understand and be committed to the type of school she/he is called to lead; will clarify roles and relations among principal, pastor, and board; and will analyze the personalities, politics, and policies of the local situation.

Reflection Questions

1. Define the types of Catholic schools you might some day administer.

2. Develop a chart listing the different types of schools. For *each* type of school—parish, interparish, diocesan, private—specify:

   * To whom is the principal directly accountable?
   * What type of school board/committee would be part of this type of school's governance? What would be the board's responsibilities?
   * What responsibilities would the principal assume for school finances?
   * What would be the process for evaluating the principal's performance? Who would participate? How often?
   * What would be the responsibilities of the pastor(s), diocese, and religious congregation for the school?
   * What would be the major administrative and governance challenges to the principal?

3. As a principal what is your relationship with the diocese? What services are provided to you?

4. What responsibility and process would the principal use to hire teachers and staff?

Resources

Brigham, F. H. 1993. *United States Catholic elementary and secondary schools 1992–93.* Washington, D.C.: National Catholic Educational Association.

Bryk, A. S., P. B. Holland, V. E. Lee, and R. A. Carriedo. 1984. *Effective Catholic schools: An exploration.* Washington, D.C.: National Catholic Educational Association.

Canon Law Society of America. 1983. *Code of canon law: Latin-English edition.* Washington, D.C.: Canon Law Society of America.

Gilbert, J. 1983. *Pastor as shepherd of the school community.* Washington, D.C.: National Catholic Educational Association.

O'Brien, J. S., ed. 1987. *A primer on educational governance in the Catholic Church.* CACE/NABE Governance Task Force. Washington, D.C.: National Catholic Educational Association.

Sheehan, L. 1990. *Building better boards.* Washington, D.C.: National Catholic Educational Association.

The author, Lourdes Sheehan, RSM, is director of the Alliance for Catholic Education at the University of Notre Dame in South Bend, Indiana.

The Principal's Role in Finance and Development

Joel Konzen, SM

Finance and Catholic school principals

Financial management and development are twin components in a single enterprise for preserving Catholic schools: assuring the viability of a school's essential activities. Financial management entails providing the funding needed to accomplish the necessary elements of the school's operation. Development encompasses planning for the adequacy of school resources. The principal needs to be prepared to take ownership and leadership in both of these tasks. Together financial management and development ensure the existence of the school and the continuation of its religious and academic mission.

Acquiring and managing the school's financial resources may be the least appealing and the most frightening and mysterious of tasks for which Catholic school principals are responsible. People aspiring to lead Catholic schools are often attracted to administration because they view it as a ministry that promotes the faith development of students, parents, and faculty (Ciriello 1993). It is common for Catholic school administrators to feel less than confident in their financial expertise (Ciriello 1991, 1992) and to bemoan their dearth of preparation for overseeing the fundamental business aspects of a school. Becoming the chief administrator of a school, nevertheless, often necessitates designing, managing, and balancing a six- or seven-figure school budget. This can be the occasion for some of the most challenging, immediate, and critical learning an aspiring or new principal is likely to encounter.

Successful handling of financial management and development responsibilities requires the principal to implement a variety of skills in both leadership and management. Bryk, Holland, Lee, and Carriedo (1984) found that effective Catholic schools had, among other qualities, principals who recognized and dealt effectively with the complex demands of their school situations. These principals were aware of and capable of addressing the diverse conditions in which their schools were expected to thrive.

Leadership behaviors which directly influence a Catholic school's viability and growth include

- establishing a vision,
- maintaining qualitative and quantitative goals,
- cultivating responsible leadership within the school,
- inculcating cooperation and productivity,
- acting decisively, and
- realizing a comprehensive plan for school improvement.

Financial management

Financial management entails two things: first, knowing the school's present and future needs and, second, mapping a strategy for funding all of those needs. It requires the principal to work according to existing policies of the diocese and in conjunction with the school's board, pastor (in parish schools), finance committee, development committee, inschool business personnel (where available), and diocesan administrators.

Burke (1984) states that "budgeting is the key to financial control" (p. 22). Beginning with a clear understanding of the mission and philosophy of the school the budgeting process seeks to establish the cost-per-pupil of operating the school and then to project the income for meeting those costs. The per-pupil costs should accurately reflect all the expenses involved in providing the school program. The principal undertakes the budgeting process in concert with an established finance committee of the parish or the school board. In parish schools, the pastor approves the final budget. In non-parish schools approval is granted by the finance committee of the school's governing group. In both cases, the principal needs to have sufficient input into the budgeting process to represent the perceived and documented needs of all school programs.

Once the budget is determined, the principal ensures that the various budgeted funding goals are met and that spending does not exceed prescribed outlays. If the principal is not successful in these two primary responsibilities, budgeted programs and personnel necessary to the school's mission will be in jeopardy.

The pastor and/or the finance committee are involved in regularly monitoring progress in maintaining an approved budget. They will want to see the budget steered along a predictable and healthy course. The principal who welcomes the assistance of members of the finance committee with expertise in financial planning and management (accountants, bankers, consultants, or corporate managers) will be at an advantage in achieving financial objectives.

A principal's insistence on systematic procedures in accounting and on acknowledging every transaction assures both the school's governing entity and the public that all resources are respected. Frequently when prudence is neglected in this area and money is mishandled, the result is a crisis in confidence, and other funding is either withheld or withdrawn. Loss of trust in the administrator's business management skills often signals impending decline for a school.

Many dioceses through their business offices are prepared to lend assistance to principals. Diocesan officials prefer helping neophyte principals with financial management rather than coming to the rescue of schools in trouble which have not availed themselves of existing resources. If no organized orientation to financial management is offered, a new principal should inquire which diocesan personnel might be called upon for help and advice. Principals should not hesitate to request assistance as needed.

Special expense considerations

Certain items deserve particular attention because of the role they play in determining the size as well as the year-to-year predictability of the annual budget.

Salaries and Benefits

Labor costs make up the greatest part of any school's budget. Some questions to consider in budgeting these costs are

- What is your long-term objective or strategy regarding compensation?
- How does your compensation package compare with other Catholic, non-public, and public schools?
- Is the salary scale in use effective or in need of revision?
- Are there compensation issues requiring attention beyond the standard scales and benefit provisions?
- Are there personnel assignments to be funded for the first time?
- How is all this addressed in this budget?

Additional Personnel

Months before the annual budget is actually approved, discussions should take place (with pastor, board, committees, and councils) about the need for additional personnel and the likelihood of being able to acquire them. Agreement should be reached on the additional personnel before the preliminary budget is drawn up.

Financial Aid

If the school has a plan for allocating tuition reductions or other grants-in-aid, a total amount of aid available and a formula for its distribution will need to be determined. A budget cannot be balanced if this figure is allowed to expand during the course of the school year. The principal will do well to rely on the services of a screening company or committee, which recommends aid amounts according to school-established criteria for all applicants. Further reasonable but firm deadlines and procedures should be in place for the dispensing of funds.

Books and Materials

Costs of replacing and purchasing new instructional materials, especially student texts, should be staggered systematically over a number of years. Ideally the outlay for these materials would be roughly comparable each year. General directions regarding appropriate review criteria and suggested replacement schedules are often provided by staff and diocesan guidelines and/or from accrediting agencies. The principal needs to work closely with the school board and professional staff to develop local guidelines to ensure a consistent process for addressing curriculum changes and their consequent materials changes.

Depreciation

An amount is normally included in the budget under the heading "Depreciation." Its purpose is to fund major repair and eventual replacement of facilities. Ideally, this revenue will be set aside in a separate plant fund or capital improvement fund. Usually, a percentage of the entire budget is designated as the depreciation amount.

Utilities

Local and extenuating circumstances (such as weather and natural disasters) from year to year can make utility costs quite volatile. Increasing use of technology in the administration and instructional aspects of the school also can significantly affect utility costs. Wise anticipation and prudent budgeting are called for in this area.

Sources of funding

Addressing Catholic school governance and finance issues for the National Congress: Catholic Schools for the 21st Century, Hocevar (1991) writes:

> Catholic schools have been resourced and financed in numerous ways by the Catholic community. These sources include: the payment of tuition; the contributions of parishioners for their parish school; the contributed salaries and services of . . . religious and lay [faculty]; diocesan, religious community, and parish services and subsidies; short-range fundraising; long-range development efforts; the contributions of Catholics, concerned citizens, and the business and corporate community to diocesan endowment campaigns; federal and state aid in the form of transportation, special educational services, textbooks, and other opportunities; and the volunteer services of a host of people whose belief in Catholic education has both inspired and supported the efforts of the schools (pp. 10–11).

The majority of funding for schools continues to be derived from tuition. Ideally, the enrollment and corresponding tuition payments would satisfy the school's operations budget, so that raised funds could be applied to special improvement projects and replacement of equipment and facilities. This is often not possible, however, because of faltering enrollments or a conscious decision to keep tuition at a level affordable to the broadest possible range of students and parents. As a result, most Catholic schools continue to rely on additional funding sources—subsidy, annual fund-raising activities, endowment/investment, or a development program—to meet some operational costs.

Tuition

Since every dollar earned through enrollment is a dollar that does not have to be raised, the first order in tuition management is assuring that enrollment exceeds or, at the very least, meets the number projected. In a very real sense, recruitment of new students is a primary element of financial stability and, as such, is one of the principal's most pressing responsibilities.

Thus, it is incumbent upon the principal to see that attention be given to retaining enrolled students. Monetti-Souply (1990) offers the following recruitment and retention strategies:

- providing welcome and orientation processes,
- monitoring carefully students' academic progress,

- offering counseling and advising services,
- responding to parent concerns in a timely and professional fashion,
- developing leadership opportunities for students,
- maintaining varied and appropriate student activities,
- reviewing regularly the curriculum to be sure it is serving the school's students well, and
- conducting exit interviews with departing students and their families.

The principal, working with the financial advisory body, determines fair policies for collecting all funds owed to the school and establishes a process for dealing with postponed or waived payments. Sometimes schools contract with a company which acts as the collector of its tuition monies (see page 114). Consistency in tuition collection is more important than the specific method employed. Principals who fail to collect owed funds abet the school's financial problems by sending a message that stipulated payments are not acutely needed—a premise that will prove lethal when the school seeks additional funds.

Subsidy

Sponsoring parishes often allocate some operating monies to their parish schools. Ideally, this support is seen by the parish to be a ministerial service provided its parishioners and others interested in a religiously based education. Often subsidy is the factor allowing the school to remain viable while charging a reasonable tuition. Dioceses, too, sometimes supply selected schools with funds for operations. Schools sponsored by religious communities may receive support through community contributions or the contributed services (less than full salaries) of community members at the school.

In the last twenty years, this form of funding has declined precipitously. Parish subsidy of Catholic schools has decreased an average of roughly 1 percent a year nationwide since 1973—from more than half a school's budget to 34 percent in 1991 (Harris 1992, Kealey 1992). Discretionary funds for all church entities are being stretched to address concerns which were unheard of or of a lower priority a generation ago. Hence, principals who rely too heavily on subsidy for bridging the gap between revenue and costs restrict the school's vision to what such limited and threatened support can finance.

Fund-Raisers

Catholic schools have long epitomized the "every-penny-counts" operation that misses no opportunity for raising funds through sales, games, or socials. In many schools, the place of bingo or an annual festival which generates significant revenue is regarded as essential. Such activities usually offer the school a social benefit, as well, by uniting parents, students, and others in garnering support.

But fund-raisers are not without their drawbacks. They require a constant resupply of dedicated volunteers. In all but the largest events, such as an auction or ball, fund-raisers secure roughly the amount of money produced the year before. Thus, while the fund-raiser is, depending on the quality of volunteer help, a somewhat stable source of funding, it is often unable to promise meaningful growth in revenue to the school.

Endowment and Foundation Income

Schools which have been able to establish an endowment, or which derive income from a diocesan or other locally established foundation, meet some of their expenses through accrued interest paid according to a set formula. The establishment of this type of funding source, based on invested principal contributed to a trust, is the sign of a mature development effort in a school or locale.

Although amounts from foundation and endowment income sources are small in the early years of their growth, they are extremely stable. An endowment for the individual school, or participation in a diocesan educational foundation, is a recommended goal for every Catholic school. These revenues are protected against the shifts in funding brought about by local economic conditions, enrollment declines, church personnel changes, and fund-raising failures. Kealey (1992) reports that 32 percent of Catholic elementary schools had established endowments by 1991.

Development

Of all the Catholic school's funding sources, a development program has the greatest potential for expanding the school's resources. It is a renewable funding source with the capacity to grow annually, even as subsidy sources may be in decline. Because it seeks funding from all those who can afford to contribute to the mission of Catholic schools, it allows the schools to keep tuition levels lower than would be possible relying on traditional income providers.

The Chicago consulting firm of Gonser, Gerber, Tinker, and Stuhr defines *development* as the "total effort on the part of the institution to

- analyze its educational or programmatic philosophy and activities,
- crystallize its objectives,
- project them into the future, and
- take the necessary steps to realize them" (Gonser et al. 1977, p. 4).

A successful development program in a Catholic school is likely to include

- a strategic or long-range plan that is drawn up by the school's board, managed by the principal, and revised at regular intervals;
- an enrollment and marketing strategy managed by the principal and a committee;
- an annual giving campaign involving mail, telephone, and face-to-face (direct) solicitation of the school's potential contributors: graduates, parents, grandparents, businesses, and friends of Catholic education;
- securing of planned gifts through such instruments as wills, trusts, and insurance policies for the sake of establishing and enlarging an endowment or foundation;
- the assistance of development professionals: a paid consultant, a member of the school's staff, or both;
- the empowerment of the school board for the purpose of skilled involvement in moving the direction of the school's plans and advancement programs;
- a comprehensive program of public relations which informs the school's constituents and larger community of the school's essential mission and the steps it is taking to realize that mission.

A primary responsibility of the principal, after having become well-informed about the details and possibilities of development programs, is to educate everyone concerned with the school—including pastor, board, financial advisers, faculty, parents, and students—about the role this mechanism can play in securing the future of the Catholic school. Once others are aware of how development works and what it can provide, the principal can plan aggressively for implementing the various components.

Development and fund raising are distinct entities with different purposes. Fund-raising efforts often entail a series of finite events. Schools whose energies are directed primarily to fund-raisers such as bingo, raffles, suppers, and candy sales usually rely on volunteer leadership and coordination for handling these events. Principals approve plans, attend events, and sometimes designate the proceeds for various needs.

A development program, on the other hand, is an ongoing, systematic effort that requires a greater commitment from the principal. Some larger Catholic schools may have an administrator whose chief responsibility is to oversee the development program; that official is generally called "president."

The role of the principal in schools without designated personnel concerned primarily with development is

- to see that a program is initiated,
- to secure capable volunteer and/or funded personnel,
- to educate all at the school about the aims and practice of development,
- to (work with a committee) to devise and implement a workable development plan (Konzen 1991).

In schools with ambitious development efforts, it is not unrealistic to project that about 40 percent of a principal's time will be spent in development-related tasks. Most principals will find that the only way they can make such a block of time available is by delegating some leadership responsibilities to others in the school. Thus, in order to advance the goals of comprehensive development, the principal may be forced—and this is not necessarily bad—to ask: Can someone on my staff handle other aspects of administration such as scheduling substitute teachers, managing attendance and health concerns, sharing in the handling of discipline matters, assisting in classroom observations, preparing weekly schedules, or being responsible for liturgy and lunchroom supervision?

Unless a principal is convinced of the need for considerable personal involvement in development projects and is willing to create time for managing the development effort, the program will be doomed to remain an add-on that is not integral to advancing the school's mission properly and profoundly. Principals can be assisted significantly by appointing a paid or volunteer development officer for the school. This person oversees much of the planning and actual operation of development efforts, thus freeing the principal to concentrate on setting goals, recruiting effective volunteers, energizing the board and its committees, and making personal calls on those who can help the school realize its development objectives.

The principal (along with the development officer, where one has been appointed) works in conjunction with a development committee. This committee can be an independent committee of carefully selected volunteers, a standing committee of the school's board, or a combination of these two groups. Together with the principal, the committee establishes annual goals and comes to agreement on methods to attain the goals. It is the principal's responsibility to lead in executing the group's plans and to report regularly on progress (La Riviere 1993).

Various publications exist which may assist principals in learning more about development's purposes and methods. Many of them are listed in the resources. In addition to the annual development conference held in conjunction with NCEA's Easter-week convention, conferences and symposia for Catholic school leaders are conducted by other sponsors throughout the year. Attendance at an NCEA convention may be the best opportunity for principals to become acquainted with the considerable resources available in development.

Technical assistance

A principal must press as persistently as necessary for the technical equipment needed to handle the school's business affairs professionally. Good computer software managed by a knowledgeable professional will aid a principal considerably in financial management and development. Keeping accurate records of incoming and outgoing monies is an absolute necessity for monitoring the budget and forecasting needed revenue. As the development program becomes more sophisticated, computer software can assist in tracking and analyzing giving patterns.

The principal sees, too, that, if financial recordkeeping is not otherwise available from existing parish administrative staff or school personnel, an individual with appropriate time and expertise undertakes the bookkeeping required for sound fiscal conduct.

Consulting services are also proving to be valuable resources for Catholic schools, especially as they forge long-range plans and move energetically toward campaigns in annual support, capital improvements, and planned giving. The principal, working with the development committee, does well to become acquainted with and to weigh carefully the advantages and disadvantages of incorporating such services.

Public relations and the principal

Public relations efforts go hand in hand with successful development programs. Catholic schools in many parts of the country are the "best-kept secrets" in the local area. Excellent programs go unacknowledged and unappreciated by the surrounding community because the school has not carefully crafted a systematic program of communication about itself. No educational institution has ever failed because of over-saturating a community with appropriate information concerning the merits of its programs. In some areas of the country professional marketing programs for Catholic schools are producing enrollments increased by 10 percent or more.

Public relations asks

❧ What do we want people to know?
❧ Who should hear the message about our school?
❧ How will we go about getting the message to them?

As the school's chief spokesperson, the principal uses every means available to inform the public about a school's history, mission, and current offerings and events. Unless their children attend the school, most people in parishes have little knowledge of the particular features of a parish school. Others in the community have even less idea of what the typical, local Catholic school does or whom it serves. Simply put, seats will go vacant as long as a school does not inform the public why those seats should be occupied. Every empty seat is lost revenue for the school and a missed opportunity for a youngster.

The principal should see that a marketing committee is established, either as an adjunct to the board or development committee or as a free-standing group. Members of the committee assist the principal in designing and implementing a thorough plan for informing all publics about the school, including parish members, parents of potential students, the business community, and the community at large. The marketing committee also takes responsibility for implementing a retention program at the school, tracking patterns of enrollment and reasons for withdrawal and then seeking to address weaknesses likely to result in removal of enrolled students.

The need for planning and evaluation

Just as Catholic colleges and universities have for decades engaged in strategic planning to ensure the academic quality and financial health of their institutions, so, too, Catholic elementary and secondary schools are beginning to initiate professional and systematic planning for and continual evaluation of their operations.

In her book on school planning Stone (1993) suggests, "Planning activities in independent schools respond to both the *need* and the *desire* to engage in strategic thinking," which "combines both creative and analytic processes, leads to the definition of broad guidelines for future direction (both new and continuing), and to specific actions to implement and assess results" (p. 10). This "strategic thinking" is basic to preparing a school for sound financial management and for development programs. This planning must take place within the context of the school's defined mission. Peter Drucker's famous quip, "If you don't know where you're going, any plan will do" (Bryson 1990, p. 93), is a reminder that unplanned evolution may bring devastating results.

Every Catholic school has a distinctive mission—one that is, ideally, updated regularly and propounded aggressively within the school community. This unique mission shapes even the subtlest notion of where the school needs to be heading and should be the basis for all planning in the school. Bryson (1990) says "developing the [mission] statement begins a habit of focusing a discussion on what is truly important" (p. 97). It is the primary mission, often expressed in simple but compelling terms, which helps school planners to focus on the most important, and hence most urgent, aspects for attention and improvement.

Vaill (1984) says that in "high-performing systems" (p. 85) members have "pictures in their heads which are strikingly congruent" (p. 86). Such organizations usually have a universally understood and agreed-upon mission. Consequently, all who are responsible for growth and direction refer to these common "pictures" for some avenue to the future.

The effective Catholic school principal takes care to assemble a group of cooperators—school board members, volunteer leadership, and school staff—who can find satisfaction in the "pictures" of where the school is headed and can energetically assist in realizing the design proposed in the school's plan. It is essential that the school's board be composed of people who bring real skills in leadership, analysis, and business. The board exists to provide advice and movement *not* ordinarily available from staff or assigned personnel. Although board members' goals should be congruent with those of the school's designated leadership, their backgrounds should not mimic those of people already at work in the school.

Once the plan is formulated, regular revisions are necessary, as is evaluation to chart the success of implementing the plan. At least once a year, a formal evaluation of progress on meeting long-range objectives should be conducted. Generally, this takes place within the context of the school board, with input sought from faculty, parents, and the public. Surveys and marketing studies can be helpful in determining whether changes brought about through planned improvements are achieving the desired effects.

Resources in print

In addition to texts mentioned elsewhere, the following resources can serve to acquaint a principal with many of the aspects entailed in finance and development responsibilities:

- Catholic School Management's bimonthly newsletter for administrators which often treats topics related to the fiscal concerns of principals.
- Planning and management guides: local bookstores and college libraries are brimming with texts that outline basic principles and practices for managers and can be adapted to the Catholic school setting. Especially helpful are publications geared toward nonprofit organizations.
- Research studies and statistical reports published through NCEA, in NCEA's *Momentum* magazine, independently as doctoral dissertations or as scholarly articles (available through electronic search services), or by the Council for the Advancement and Support of Education (CASE). NCEA publishes updated statistics on Catholic elementary and secondary school finances every two years.
- Publications from professional organizations: NCEA's Fastback series on many aspects of development; CASE's monthly *Currents* and topical treatments of public relations, giving campaigns, and other development concerns; the National Center for Nonprofit Boards' newsletter and books; planning and accounting guides from the National Association of Independent Schools; and *Ideas and Perspectives*, a newsletter from Independent School Management.
- *Effective Funding of Catholic Schools* by Thompson and Flynn (1988), which offers research and methodology on increasing the extraordinary funding (beyond tuition and subsidies) for Catholic schools.
- *Building Better Boards* by Lourdes Sheehan, RSM (1990), and other board-related materials from NCEA.

Quality as the touchstone

A reliable starting point for a beginning principal is to be certain that the education offered at the school is worth at least as much as the tuition charged. While a host of recent studies (Bryk 1984, Chubb 1990, Coleman 1987, Yeager

1985) have confirmed that Catholic schools in general offer an environment and academic preparation in many ways preferable or superior to that in other schools with a greater per-pupil cost, it cannot be assumed that every Catholic school automatically delivers such premium performance for its students. The principal, as well as the school board and, as applicable, the pastor, serve as the guardians and constructive critics to ensure that the school is offering a Catholic education of the highest quality to all its students. Such deliberative action goes a long way to guarantee that funds sought in the name of and on behalf of the school support a worthy educational opportunity. Further, careful stewardship demands that all resources be treated fairly, ethically, and imaginatively to enhance the mission of the institution.

Assuring quality experiences in all aspects of the school's operations will easily attract the cooperators and volunteers necessary for success in finance and development efforts. The principal who is pursuing a vision of excellence for all the school's features has no time for lamenting the lack of interest or support from one constituency or another because that principal will be busy creating whatever is lacking and, in the process, creating the means whereby the school will not just survive but will become exemplary.

Reflection Questions

1. What resources will you need to prepare yourself and others to understand and lead in Catholic school financial management and development?

2. In order to construct and maintain the school budget, how will you see the activities of financial management and development as complementary?

3. How can working with finance and development committees enhance the principal's budgeting abilities?

4. How can the variety of funding sources be tapped for availability in the school's operations?

5. Why is a development program unlikely to succeed unless others at the school are sympathetic to its aims and methods?

6. Why is delegation of duties often important to principals embarking on a development program in their schools?

7. Principals need not and should not "go it alone" in the areas of financial management and development. Explain.

8. How is public relations pivotal in maintaining the viability of and engendering growth in Catholic schools?

9. What is the role of student recruitment and retention in advancing a financially healthy operation for Catholic schools?

10. A principal without a comprehensive long-range plan for the school is apt to feel vulnerable and unsteady. Explain.

11. In what sense is *quality* the umbrella under which so many of the school's plans and hopes are assembled?

Resources

Brigham, F. H. 1993. *United States Catholic elementary and secondary schools 1992–93.* Washington, D.C.: National Catholic Educational Association.

Bryk, A. S., P. B. Holland, V. E. Lee, and R. A. Carriedo. 1984. *Effective Catholic schools: An exploration.* Washington, D.C.: National Catholic Educational Association.

Bryson, J. M. 1990. *Strategic planning for public and nonprofit organizations.* San Francisco: Jossey-Bass Publishers.

Burke, R. 1984. *Elementary school finance manual.* Washington, D.C.: National Catholic Educational Association.

Bushman, E. M., and G. J. Sparks, eds. 1990. *The Catholic school administrator: A book of readings.* Portland, Ore: Catholic Leadership Co.

Catholic schools face fiscal facts. 1993. Editorial. *America* 169(18):3.

Chubb, J. E., and T. M. Moe. 1990. *Politics, markets, and America's schools.* Washington, D.C.: The Brookings Institution.

Ciriello, M. J. 1991. *Catholic principals' survey concerning their role and the future of Catholic education in the Archdiocese of Boston.* Boston: Catholic Schools Office.

———. 1992. *Attitudes of Catholic school administrators of the Diocese of Honolulu concerning their role and the future of Catholic education on the Islands.* Honolulu, Hawaii: Catholic School Department.

Ciriello, M. J., and J. J. Convey. 1993. Catholic higher education and diocesan school departments: Collaborating to strengthen leadership. *Current Issues in Catholic Higher Education* 14(1):34–39.

Coleman, J. S., and T. Hoffer. 1987. *Public and private high schools: The impact of communities.* New York: Basic Books.

Donaldson, F. 1991. *Catholic school publications: Unifying the image.* Washington, D.C.: National Catholic Educational Association.

Gary, B. S. 1986. *Seeking foundation grants.* Washington, D.C.: National Catholic Educational Association.

Gonser, Gerber, Tinker, and Stuhr. 1988. *On Development.* Chicago.

Guerra, M. J. 1993. *Dollars and sense: Catholic high schools and their finances 1992.* Washington, D.C.: National Catholic Educational Association.

Harris, J. C. 1992. Is the American Catholic Church getting out of the elementary school business? *Chicago Studies* 31(1):81–92.

———. 1994. Catholics can too afford schools. *America* 170(8):22–24.

Hocevar, R. 1991. Catholic school governance. In *Catholic school governance and finance.* Washington, D.C.: National Catholic Educational Association.

Kealey, R. 1992. *United States Catholic elementary schools and their finances 1991.* Washington, D.C.: National Catholic Educational Association.

Konzen, J. 1991. *The role of the principal in development.* Washington, D.C.: National Catholic Educational Association.

La Riviere, A. 1993. *The development council: Cornerstone for success.* Washington, D.C.: National Catholic Educational Association.

McCormick, M. T. 1994. Close, but no cigar. *America* 170(8):24–26.

Monetti-Souply, M. 1990. *A year-round recruitment and retention plan*. Washington, D.C.: National Catholic Educational Association.

Oldenburg, R. L. 1991. *Conducting the phonathon*. Washington, D.C.: National Catholic Educational Association.

Peterson, J. 1990. *How to hire a development officer: From defining needs to ensuring successful performance*. Washington, D.C.: National Catholic Educational Association.

Sheehan, L. 1990. *Building better boards*. Washington, D.C.: National Catholic Educational Association.

————. 1991. Governance. In *Catholic school governance and finance*. Washington, D.C.: National Catholic Educational Association.

Stangl, A. 1990. *The one-person development office*. Washington, D.C.: National Catholic Educational Association.

Stone, S. C. 1987. *Strategic planning for independent schools*. Boston: National Association of Independent Schools.

————. 1993. *Shaping strategy: Independent school planning in the '90s*. Boston: National Association of Independent Schools.

Tedesco, J. 1991. *Catholic schools and volunteers: A planned involvement*. Washington, D.C.: National Catholic Educational Association.

Thompson, L. A., and J. A. Flynn. 1988. *Effective funding of Catholic schools*. Kansas City, Mo.: Sheed and Ward.

Tracy, M. 1990. *Steps in direct solicitation: Preparation, presentation, and follow-up*. Washington, D.C.: National Catholic Educational Association.

Vaill, P. B. 1984. The purposing of high-performing systems. In *Leadership and organizational culture*, ed. T. J. Sergiovanni and J. E. Corbally, 85–104. Urbana: University of Illinois Press.

Yeager, R. J., P. L. Benson, M. J. Guerra, and B. V. Manno. 1985. *The Catholic high school: A national portrait*. Washington, D.C.: National Catholic Educational Association.

The author, Joel Konzen, SM, is the president/principal at Saint Michael's Academy in Austin, Texas.

These organizations offer administrative resources, workshops, publications, or consultants:

Catholic Education Marketing Initiative
629 N. Fairview Avenue
St. Paul, MN 55104

Catholic Leadership Company
5470 S.W. Dover Loop
Portland, OR 97225

Catholic School Management
24 Cornfield Lane
Madison, CT 06443

Council for Advancement and Support of Education (CASE)
Suite 400
11 Dupont Circle
Washington, DC 20036-1261

Independent School Management
1315 N. Union Street
Wilmington, DE 19806-2594

Institute of School and Parish Development
Suite 703
2026 St. Charles Avenue
New Orleans, LA 70130

These organizations, among others, contract with Catholic schools in the management of tuition payments or financial aid screening:

F.A.C.T.S. Tuition Management
P. O. Box 67037
Lincoln, NE 68506

SMART Tuition Management Services
Suite 2300
95 Wall Street
New York, NY 10005

Tuition Aid Data Services
Suite 104
2305 Ford Parkway
St. Paul, MN 55116

Critical
Relationships
◆◆◆

The Role of the Pastor in the Parish with a School

Msgr. Francis X. Barrett

Introduction

The Catholic school traditionally has been a pillar for Catholic parishes in the United States. Throughout the century, Catholic schools have been exposing children to the truths of the faith as well as instructing them in all areas of knowledge. However, the justification for establishing and maintaining Catholic schools has taken a subtle shift. In the beginning of the century the purpose of the parish Catholic school was to provide youth an education which would "maintain the integrity of their faith in a culture that was predominantly Protestant" (Weakland 1994, p. xi). Today the Catholic school stands not so much as a hedge against "Protestantism," but rather as a response to the secularism, materialism, consumerism, individualism, and fragmentation of knowledge so prevalent in modern American society (Heft 1991). Much of the research shows that the Catholic school has succeeded admirably in its mission to train the mind, soul, and body (Coleman 1987, Convey 1992).

Nevertheless, this success has not come cheaply. Buetow (1985) notes that from the start willing, often heroic, sacrifices and determination of clergy, religious, and laity built the schools. Today, every pastor continues to face the ongoing challenge of increased school operating costs. This formidable demand on the leadership of the pastor is critical to the viable future of the schools. These schools, which have demonstrated their effectiveness in transmitting the truths of our faith and passing on the faith to succeeding generations, are needed more than ever for the welfare of the Catholic faith.

Indeed, the future vitality of the Catholic parish is linked to the quality of religious education and formation of its members. Greeley (1992) states emphatically: "The American Catholic parish is one of the most successful attempts at community formation human ingenuity ever devised and the parochial school is the most successful instrument yet developed to link Catholics with parish community" (p. 43).

In earlier research Greeley (1966) found that those educated in a Catholic school are most likely to assume leadership positions in the Church as adults. Twenty-five years later that fact can still be validated with even a cursory survey inquiring about the educational experiences of current active parishioners (e.g., lectors, eucharistic ministers, ushers, parish council members, leaders of organizations, and Catholic school teachers). Generally these people attended Catholic school when one was available to them.

The proven effectiveness of the Catholic school in fulfilling the Church's mission is a strong argument to present to parishioners. Fostering an attitude that the school is a treasure—a resource and opportunity for serving the needs of the local community and the larger Church—rather than blaming it when other parish programs seem inadequately funded will go a long way in building the kingdom. Greeley (1992) notes the secret for the future of Catholic schools is in parish resources—human, organizational, and financial. His "radical" idea is for pastors to work with laity, making them full partners in decision making and giving them more responsibility for the future of the school.

Keeping in mind the pivotal place the pastor holds in the parish, his commitment to the school and its mission is critical to the life and future of the school. The following points are offered to provide some guidelines for a pastor's interactions with the school which support the school's mission. These ideas are organized around the various ways a pastor can be present to the school community.

Spiritual presence

If the school is to fulfill its role in the parish community, it must be faithful to its mission to prepare pupils for a participatory role in parish life and in the Church of the future. The pastor exhibits leadership when he works with the principal, faculty, and director of religious education (DRE) to ensure that a mission statement is prepared for the school that clearly spells out the meaning of "Catholic." This brief statement about the purpose and core values of the school then provides a natural benchmark from which to plan, implement, and evaluate all aspects of school life, including religious and academic instruction, sacramental preparation, and liturgical celebration. Further fostering an understanding and commitment to the mission of the school in all those associated with the school community is crucial.

In cooperation with the principal, the pastor has a serious responsibility to ensure the competence of those who teach religion. Pastors who visit classrooms to observe religion instruction will gain first-hand experience and assurance that the program is being appropriately conducted. This information will serve him well when parishioners inquire about the Catholic identity of the school. Ideally, all the priests of the parish will teach religion class or classes in the school on a regular basis. The presence of the priest in the classroom affords the students a valuable opportunity to get to know "Father" on a more informal and human level. Many vocations have been fostered through such encounters.

As the spiritual leader of the parish, the pastor has an obligation to closely monitor the children's preparation for all sacraments. While the DRE and the principal will tend to the details and appropriate arrangements for First Penance and First Eucharist, the pastor's visits to the classroom are needed to ensure that the children are comfortable with these important events in their spiritual lives and are well prepared for them. If Confirmation is administered while the children are in grade school, the pastor again should be involved. However, depending on diocesan guidelines and parish procedures, this involvement may take a form with less classroom interaction. Active pastor involvement with parents in the course of sacramental preparation sends a strong message about the priority the sacraments have for the pastor.

By virtue of its mission, every Catholic school should provide opportunities for prayer and sacramental reception for all its members. No doubt, the principal ensures that prayer is an integral part of the school day. The pastor will want to familiarize himself with these routines and ensure that the principal emphasizes the importance of and expectations about prayer in the school program at the faculty meeting beginning the school year. It is important that all teachers understand and implement the common practices of prayer throughout the day. On another note, the teachers themselves need opportunities to pray together in order to grow in their spiritual lives and to form a vibrant faith community within the school. When the pastor celebrates liturgy with the faculty and/or participates in retreat or similar experiences, he is demonstrating both his interest and his concern for the faith-life of the adult community involved in the school.

Regularly scheduled eucharist for the children is an important part of their education and spiritual development. The principal should ensure that the teachers have the skills to prepare the children for as full and meaningful participation as their age and capabilities permit. This liturgy is an exceptional opportunity afforded the pastor (and other priests) to speak directly to the children about God. To take full advantage of this powerful formation opportunity, the celebrant will want to prepare a short homily that uses language that speaks to the personal experiences of the children. The frequency and group composition of the school eucharistic celebration is the subject of debate. Ideally the pastor and principal will work together to develop a schedule that allows for whole school, grade cluster, and individual class liturgies. A scheduled weekly liturgy for a major division of the student body will provide enough experience in the course of a year for the children to feel comfortable and to learn to be appropriately involved and attentive. Such a liturgy, if published in the parish bulletin, encourages parent and adult parish participation. This is one way parents can participate directly in their child's religious education. The wider parish will also have an opportunity to pray with its youth and to witness firsthand some results of their education.

Other religious activities such as Penance Services, Stations of the Cross, and May Procession will depend on the customs of the diocese and parish. In any case, the pastor who systematically works with the principal to plan and provide for the spiritual development of the students and faculty will find the effort rewarded. He will have a realistic idea of what is happening in the school, will be able to converse with conviction about the education of the children, and will have the satisfaction of knowing that he is seen as an interested, caring spiritual leader by all associated with the school community.

Financial presence

If there is one way the pastor has been traditionally present and involved in the school, it is in the financial realm. Because of this sometimes overwhelming responsibility, even a pastor who is completely supportive of the Catholic school cannot help but occasionally imagine how much less complicated life would be if he had the parish school subsidy available for other uses.

In any sound financial planning the first step is to develop a realistic school budget. Most dioceses have guidelines and processes to help the pastor and principal with this important task. As determined by local practice, the prepared budget is submitted for approval to the appropriate parties which may include the pastor, principal, school board, finance committee, parish council, or any combination of these.

Before the budget is finalized for approval, those preparing it need to know the amount of parish subsidy that the school can expect. This figure will dictate the tuition rate and amount of fund raising necessary for a balanced budget. After the budget is approved, the pastor and principal (ideally in conjunction with a committee of parishioners and parents) take the lead in establishing processes for fund raising and tuition collection.

Sound business practice dictates that each year the tuition be raised at least sufficiently to account for the rate of inflation and to provide for the salary needs of the teachers. Pastors and financial committees have found that skipping a tuition increase one year often only delays the "pain" momentarily. Frequently the following year's larger-than-usual increase has a negative impact on the entire school community. There should be a clear policy on tuition aid, since this is generally a line-item in the budget. Obviously this policy will depend on local circumstances but needs to be spelled out in advance.

School fund-raising efforts, such as Christmas card and candy sales, need careful thought. The pastor and principal working together and in conjunction with the school board will try to keep such sales to a minimum, especially if the children are involved. Limiting such events to only one per school year is ideal.

For the school to become less dependent on ordinary parish income and fund-raising activities, some longer-range planning and strategies need to be put into place to secure ongoing funds. "Development" is the term associated with these types of activities. The principal and pastor would do well to form a small committee of interested persons to explore possibilities and strategies. Some successful strategies are asking people to sponsor specific individual students, to contribute to a scholarship fund, or to contribute to a school endowment fund. For seed money some pastors are able to put aside a few hundred dollars a month which can be spared from parish income. When invested in an endowment fund, this relatively small amount soon grows to a substantial sum. At the same time, alumni, friends, and local businesses should be asked to contribute to this endowment fund.

Raising the money is one thing; spending it wisely is another. A budget is a mere piece of paper if it does not truly govern the fiscal operation of the school. The principal, who is charged with the operation of the budget, will be greatly supported by the pastor who includes a quarterly review of school finances on the agenda of the parish finance committee. Systematic monitoring avoids unpleasant surprises at the year's end.

The other side of prudent financial planning for the school is a lively marketing and recruitment program. The school promotion campaign is critical to obtaining the resources for a quality curriculum and to keeping costs manageable. Depending on the size of the school, a full- or part-time public relations coordinator is needed to assist the principal in promoting the school. Every effort should be made to let the community know what the school is doing. Each year the National Catholic Educational Association (NCEA) provides valuable resources for both public relations and marketing which the pastor can urge the principal to obtain and use to the advantage of the school.

Another topic the school community should discuss is enrollment. From a financial perspective every school has fixed costs which must be paid whether there are 100 or 300 children in the school. Having an enrollment that allows for a reasonable pupil-teacher ratio while spreading the costs among a larger number of children is the ideal situation.

Aside from the financial perspective, the more important question is the MISSION question. For whom does the school exist? Who is to be educated in the school? Obviously in a parish school it is parishioners first of all. After all, the parish subsidizes the school. But, if there is room, should Catholic non-parishioners be admitted? If so, at what tuition? Will the "home" parish assist you with the per-pupil cost differential? If there is additional room, should non-Catholics be admitted? Should they pay the total per-pupil cost or should this be considered part of the parish's evangelization effort? After consultation with the appropriate groups—board, parish council, finance committee, and principal—it is the pastor who must decide these matters. The diocese may have guidelines for such situations.

When there are openings, at first glance it seems preferable to have a tuition-paying student in a seat rather than having the seat empty. But the mission and community spirit that are the heart and soul of the school need to be nurtured by persons who genuinely value and seek the kind of education the Catholic school is offering. Neither the child nor the school is well served if the parents do not wholeheartedly embrace the basic values and goals of the school. Therefore, regardless of enrollment numbers, no child should be admitted until there is a clear indication from the parents or guardians that they are willing to support the child's educational efforts through participation in parent-teacher conferences, embracing the philosophy and mission of the school, supporting the homework, discipline, and (as applicable) uniform policies, etc. Cooperative, active parents are critical to the child's academic success. Furthermore, calling all parents to their responsibility to be active participants in their children's education is entirely consistent with a long history of papal encyclicals and other church documents which recognize that parents bear the primary responsibility for their children's education (*Declaration on Christian Education* 1966, *Code of Canon Law* 1983, Leo XIII 1887, Pius XI 1929). Indeed, this tenet returns us to the historical purpose for Catholic schools which was to help parents protect their children from the blatantly Protestant influence found in the public schools of the time. That concern seems mild compared to the more pervasive threats of materialism, secularism, and atheism that plague the modern family. Catholic schools that support family values are needed today more than ever.

Social presence

Probably the most difficult thing for the pastor is to fit the seemingly endless round of school events into his already-full menu of parish responsibilities. Yet nothing cheers the students, teachers, and parents more than the pastor's presence at things that he "doesn't have" to attend. Budget meetings and religious events are the ordinary times which call the pastor to exert his leadership. But his presence at science fair exhibits, spelling bees, and mathathons indicates a different level of concern and involvement that pleases the school community.

Such informal activities as merely visiting the school building, stopping to talk to the children on the playground during recess, strolling the hallways, and visiting the cafeteria send powerful messages to all involved with the school that the pastor, as busy as he is, still has time for the "little ones." I recommend that the pastor consider reading to the children during National Reading Week. It gives him a chance to appear in a different light to the children, and they love it.

In addition, there are always auxiliary groups such as Booster Clubs, Mothers' Guild, and the Parent Association. These people give generously of their time. Often their efforts support the parish as well because they contribute to keeping the costs of the school manageable. It is not unreasonable for them to hope that the pastor will attend their annual dinner or other major event.

Some participation in major faculty socials is also important. Generally, the teachers appreciate the pastor's presence at the Christmas dinner or other such events. Finally, the graduation ceremonies provide a unique opportunity to speak on the value of the school and the excellent work of faculty and students.

While all these ideas seem to require a large amount of time, it doesn't play out that way. Most of these suggestions require little more than an hour and happen only a few times a year. The results are worth the effort because the pastor is contributing to the self-esteem of a major sector of the parish, thus promoting a stronger sense of parish spirit.

Parish presence

It is absolutely essential that the school be integrated into parish life. It would be contrary to all the values and mission of the parish and school to allow the relationship to be perceived as a "them" and "us" situation. The parish bulletin is a simple vehicle that sends the message that the school is important and contributing to the vitality of the parish. The pastor should see that there is space reserved in the bulletin and arrange with the principal to have informative school news printed every week.

The children in the school should be encouraged to be involved in parish activities. The number of ways they can be present to the parish is limited only by their time and the imagination of the adults who are working with them. Some examples of ways elementary children have been involved in parish activities are serving at liturgies; helping around the sacristy; stuffing envelopes and parish bulletins; shoveling snow; raking leaves; cleaning the parish grounds; helping with child care during Sunday liturgies; sending cards to shut-ins; singing at parish functions; assisting the elderly of the parish with shopping, dog walking, or letter writing; collecting toys for the less fortunate; and bagging and delivering clothing and canned food during the holidays.

The children's experience at school liturgies should equip them to eventually assume positions as parish lector and commentator. Encouraging participation in parish life fosters an attitude of service and builds lifelong habits. It is never too soon to teach children their responsibility to share in the stewardship of time and talent. The pastor who publicly acknowledges and encourages such activities is fostering the active, concerned future adult parishioner and is contributing to a strong and vibrant parish community.

Another way the pastor may strengthen the parish-school relationship is to invite and appoint the principal and/or teachers to be members of parish committees. In this way, he as well as active parishioners who may not have children in the school can share viewpoints and learn from one another.

The pastor influences the school and the parish through appointments to the finance council, parish council, and school board. To allow for a broader exchange of views and to allow the diverse perspectives of the parish to surface, all such groups should be composed of persons who represent a wide spectrum of the parish. Particularly in the case of the school board, appointing only those families with children in the school would limit the outlook of the group and unnecessarily isolate it from other parish concerns.

Intellectual presence

As practical and important as the pastor's financial expertise and contribution is, it is not the most important offering he gives to the parish school. He brings his experience in life and ministry, and his awareness of the parish expectations for the school. To share these insights requires his meeting with the principal and faculty face-to-face periodically.

In order to benefit from the insights of the principal on all aspects of the parish, the pastor will want to include the principal in the parish staff/team meetings. In addition, the pastor needs to meet regularly with the principal about school affairs. A shared cup of coffee once a week is an excellent and informal way to make sure everyone is on the same track. Such scheduled meetings need not be formal; indeed some casual conversations can accomplish the same purpose. However, it is far better to have regularly scheduled meetings so that both pastor and principal can adequately anticipate upcoming events and prepare items of mutual interest and concern about the school. Regularly scheduled meetings of as short as thirty minutes a week will go a long way toward establishing a normal rhythm of ongoing communication that will hopefully avoid crisis situations and make both feel more at ease when that inevitable school "problem" issue arises. Naturally, the pastor should make it clear that he is available for an ad hoc meeting if a problem arises. In this case, he should ensure that, if, possible, he is thoroughly briefed in advance by the principal and has time to consider the facts. He is, after all, the court of last appeal.

The pastor will want to attend some faculty meetings or at least that part of faculty meetings where the agenda calls for discussion of religiously oriented topics or items relating to school policy. These are important to his effective functioning as an informed leader of the parish. The principal will brief the pastor on agenda items and arrange the time and content of meetings to maximize his involvement.

Through his normal communication with the principal and his attendance at faculty meetings, the pastor can clearly communicate to principal and faculty his and the parish's expectations for the school. In turn the pastor will hear the perspectives of those most closely involved with the school.

Finally, the pastor should make sure that there is an annual session to review short- and long-range plans for the school. He should plan this review with the principal and include curriculum, personnel, and physical plant aspects of the school operation. Depending on the structures in the parish, this process might also be planned in conjunction with the parish school board. Every good school must be forward looking. There is no stronger team than a pastor working cooperatively with the principal for the future of the school.

The pastor and a regional school

It is becoming more common to have joint or regional schools sponsored by several parishes. Such schools present a unique challenge to the pastors involved. It is difficult to write in detail about these situations since often each such school has it own particular constitution. Some general thoughts do seem to be in order.

The pastor should choose his parish representatives to the regional school's board with great care. He should not choose them because they agree with him, but rather because they are interested in the school and have something to offer to the board. The scheduled meetings of the board should have priority on the pastor's calendar. Not only should he attend, he should have looked at the agenda in advance and prepared himself for the meeting.

Many of the points made in "Pastor in a Parish with a School" apply to a regional school. However, because there are several pastors involved, it is important that they meet and coordinate among themselves when they will visit the school, who will take the lead in sacramental preparations, when each will celebrate the eucharist for the school, and when they will provide the Rite of Reconciliation. Unless the pastors discuss these and other school-related issues, they will tend to avoid involvement on the premise that another pastor is closer or has more children in the school. Over time this assumption could unwittingly create undue stress and perhaps feelings of estrangement for those who work in the school.

While it is more difficult in a regional school to establish a parish-school relationship, it is not impossible. Every issue of the parish bulletin should carry news from "our" school. The pastor should make it his business to talk to the principal and visit the school regularly. The several pastors involved need to plan their visits in advance to avoid disruption. Certainly, the children from each pastor's parish will look for his presence. The parents will also be grateful for his efforts. Make sure they are not disappointed.

Reflection Questions

1. In the light of the historical shift in the broad purpose for the existence of Catholic schools, complete the following sentence: The typical Catholic parish school today differs from the parish school I knew as a child in many ways because. . . . What are your feelings about these changes?

2. Comment on this statement: The need for Catholic schools is greater than it has been at any time in this century.

3. Spiritual Presence: What reaction do you have to the description of the pastor as the spiritual leader of the school?

4. Financial Presence: Money issues have always plagued Catholic schools. What specific skills are particularly needed to ensure the financial stability of the typical Catholic parish school?

5. In light of the arguments stated, comment on the principle that "parents are the primary educators of their children" and that the school has a responsibility to call forth parents' participation in their children's education.

6. Social Presence: Considering the demands of the typical total parish, realistically assess the points made in this section with respect to practical "do-ability" for the typical pastor.

7. Parish Presence: With a view to strengthening the relationship between the parish and the school, what additional ideas would you add to the ones already presented?

8. Intellectual Presence: Comment on the statement, The pastor who understands and utilizes collaboration and cooperation will multiply his influence throughout the parish.

9. Regional Schools: What are the unique leadership issues for both the pastors and the principal involved with regional schools?

10. How does a school with a large percentage of non-Catholics fulfill the expected mission of the Catholic school?

Resources

Abbott, W. M., ed. 1966. *Declaration on Christian education (Gravissimum educationis).* In *The documents of Vatican II*, trans. Joseph Gallagher. New York: The Guild Press.

Buetow, H. A. 1988. *The Catholic school: Its roots, identity, and future.* New York: Crossroad Publishing Company.

Canon Law Society of America. 1983. *Code of canon law: Latin-English edition.* Washington, D.C.: Canon Law Society of America.

Coleman, J. 1987. *Public and private high schools: The impact of communities.* New York: Basic Books.

Convey, J. J. 1992. *Catholic schools make a difference.* Washington, D.C.: National Catholic Educational Association.

Greeley, A. M. 1966. *The education of Catholic Americans.* Chicago: Aldine Publishing Company.

———. 1992. A modest proposal for the reform of Catholic schools. Summarized in *National Congress: Catholic Schools for the 21st Century: Executive Summary*, eds. M. Guerra, R. Haney, and R. Kealey. Washington, D.C.: National Catholic Educational Association.

Heft, J. 1991. Catholic identity and the Church. In *What makes a Catholic school Catholic?*, ed. F. D. Kelly, 14–21. Washington, D.C.: National Catholic Educational Association.

Leo XIII. 1887, 1979. Common duties and interests. In *Education: Papal teachings*, by the Benedictine Monks of Solesemes, trans. A. Robeschini. Boston: Daughters of St. Paul.

Pius IX. 1929, 1979. Education of the redeemed man. In *Education: Papal teachings*, by the Benedictine Monks of Solesemes, trans. A. Robeschini. Boston: Daughters of St. Paul.

Weakland, R. G. 1994. Foreword in *From the heart of the American Church*, by D. J. O'Brien. Maryknoll, N.Y.: Orbis Books.

The author, Msgr. Francis X. Barrett, is pastor of Holy Guardian Angels Parish in Reading, Pennsylvania

The Relationship of the Superintendent with the Pastor

Rev. John A. Thomas, Ph.D.

Introduction

Rather than discuss the theoretical or ideal situation, this chapter intends to present a realistic picture of the role of the superintendent working with the pastor who has a parish school. Succinctly put, that relationship can be summed up in one word: ADVISOR. This relationship is specified by the *Code of Canon Law*. This chapter will briefly explore the ramifications of the code for Catholic schools, the characteristics of a network versus a system of schools, the influence and expertise of the superintendent, and characteristics of the pro-school pastor.

The *Code of Canon Law*

Many might wonder why a chapter addressing the relationship of the superintendent to the pastor would start with a discussion of the *Code of Canon Law*. Turning to the code is not simply theoretical or philosophical but for very practical reasons. The code stipulates how the Catholic Church functions in its structure, organization, and governance. Despite our own preferred model of the Church, or our possible preference for more democratic participation, the fact remains that the current Catholic Church functions essentially as a hierarchy or monarchy. The Catholic Church is organized into a system of dioceses each headed by a bishop. The code specifies the legislative, judicial, and executive authority of the bishop as the head of his diocese. Simply stated, the bishop's authority is much like that of a king within a monarchy. The code states that the bishop is the sole legislator and final decision maker on all issues pertaining to his diocese. It is by virtue of the *Code of Canon Law* that the bishop's intent shapes the structure of the diocese. Needing and relying on the expertise of others in governing the diocese, the bishop will delegate some executive authority to others for particular tasks: vicars administer specific areas within dioceses, often superintendents are hired to oversee the schools, and pastors run parishes. The bishop also employs boards and commissions but they are, by virtue of the code, consultative and advisory. Such groups may recommend and propose legislation but they may not enact it (O'Brien 1987a).

Canon 802 stipulates that the diocesan bishop is to see that "schools imparting an education imbued with the Christian spirit" are made available (Coriden 1985). Provost notes that the bishop has special authority and responsibility for the Catholic schools within the diocese. In particular, the bishop sets direction for education within the guidelines set by the national conference of bishops. He also must watch over the faith and morals and the quality of religion teachers in all schools in his diocese (O'Brien 1987a).

Only the bishop has the authority to decide and determine how the schools of the diocese will be organized and governed. Based on the church model of sub-hierarchies, often the superintendent becomes a "sub-monarch" which is usually described as the superintendent having participation in the authority of the bishop. The extent of power delegated to the superintendent will be determined by the extent of centralization the bishop desires and the amount of authority the bishop allows the superintendent.

One model is to fashion a highly centralized school system similar to a public school system in which the bishop would direct the superintendent to act as the chief operating officer. By vesting both authority and power in the superintendent, the bishop would also expect the pastors and principals to be bound by the superintendent's directives concerning the schools. However, very few bishops establish such a centralized model.

The model bishops more often choose is not to deal with the schools directly but to see them as part of the parish structure. In this situation the focus is on the system of parishes headed by pastors with a direct line of accountability to and authority from the bishop. Canon 519 of the revised *Code of Canon Law* states that:

> the pastor is the proper shepherd of the parish entrusted to him, exercising pastoral care in the community entrusted to him under the authority of the diocesan bishop in whose ministry of Christ he has been called to share; . . . he carries out for his community the duties of teaching, sanctifying, and governing . . . (Coriden 1985).

By virtue of the code the pastor becomes a "sub-monarch" in his own parish with similar decision-making power at the parish level that the bishop has at the diocesan level. In this model, when the school is seen as part of the parish, the pastor has responsibility for the school with no direct line of accountability to the superintendent.

This latter model is not without problems. With no real leverage with pastors on school matters, the only recourse left to the superintendent is persuasion. Day in and day out the system is thus advisory and not deliberative. In other words the superintendent is an advisor to the pastor, rather than a "boss." So in those circumstances when, for any reason, the pastor chooses to ignore the superintendent's directives, the participated authority granted by the bishop to both the pastor and the superintendent is upset. The extreme way to address such cases calls for a formal appeal from either the pastor or the superintendent to the bishop to settle the difference. Needless to say, this can be unpleasant for all parties.

Network versus system

Today's diocesan parish schools are more appropriately called a "network" rather than a "system." (I would like to take credit for this insight, but the credit belongs to Father Sullivan, a former superintendent.) To clarify this idea of network as opposed to system, let us examine the differences. A system is concerned with the flow of power and authority. Usually that power allows for coercion and frequently also controls finances. A network is loose; it is not concerned with power, authority, or money.

Ordinarily, the individual Catholic school controls finances. Consequently the power of decision making is at the local not diocesan level. This fact alone gravely curtails any power the superintendent may think he or she has. Catholic parish schools simply do not have a neat flow of power from the superintendent to the local principal. The intermediary with both money and power is the pastor. Therefore the Catholic Church has a network or loose confederation of parish schools rather than a centralized system. In this regard, Catholic schools have long practiced a concept of administration that American public schools are slowly beginning to appreciate: site-based management.

Recognizing the schools as a "network" with site-based decision making supports the maxim: "Power asserted is influence denied; power denied is influence asserted." The most influential superintendent is the one who denies his or her power. When the pastor perceives that the superintendent denies his or her power, the situation is ripe for the superintendent to be what he or she should be: the chief advisor to the pastor on matters involving the school.

Superintendent's influence as advisor

The superintendent, who is professionally trained in educational issues, must be supremely knowledgeable about the schools and must put that knowledge at the service of the bishop and pastor. The superintendent, first, serves as the bishop's chief advisor on matters regarding the schools of the diocese. In reality the superintendent should stand in the same role in relation to the pastor as to the bishop.

Some would demean the idea of the superintendent as merely an advisor to the pastor. They believe that only if the superintendent has power over the pastor can he or she be effective. This essay takes the opposite position. Even Henry Kissinger, as secretary of state, had little direct power, which always resided with the president. But who would say that he did not have a very influential position? The superintendent needs to be the chief advisor to the pastor. He or she does not need power over the pastor.

The superintendent is chief advisor because the pastor usually has a local person, the principal, to advise him about schools and to see to their daily operation. The superintendent's role is to help the pastor find and select that principal. The pastor may also consult the superintendent to check on the principal's advice about the school. Finally and more frequently, the superintendent will work directly with the principal in administration of the school.

What is the limit of the advice-giving role of the superintendent in relation to the pastor? Philosophically, there is no limit. However, the farther the superintendent strays from school expertise, the more his or her credibility as a wise advisor is stretched. The real limit in an advice-giving role is the personal knowledge, wisdom, and accumulated experience in school-related situations the superintendent has attained.

Once the idea of the superintendent as chief advisor to the pastor is settled, then the advisory role can come to the fore. What happens when the pastor chooses not to interact with the superintendent, even to the point of not wanting the superintendent to stop by for a chat about the school? The *Code of Canon Law* is the guide. The care of souls in teaching, governing, and sanctifying those people is the task of the pastor under the bishop. The bishop, not the superintendent, is responsible for seeing that a man of suitable talent and temperament is assigned to a parish. Ordinarily, it is not the superintendent's role to participate in the decision of who is appointed pastor. (However, an advisory role in this area is congruent with the thesis of this essay.) If the person the bishop entrusts with a parish with a school has a deaf ear or is hostile to the superintendent, then so be it. The superintendent ought not take it personally.

The following diagram modeling how a diocese might be organized illustrates the influence and effectiveness of the superintendent. According to this diagram the relationship between the pastor and principal is clear. In the event that the superintendent tells the principal one thing and the pastor wishes something different, the diagram indicates the direct line of authority between the pastor and principal. Therefore the pastor's directives are to be followed.

The superintendent is called on to believe deeply in the principle of subsidiarity, which means that which can be accomplished by the initiative and industry of one group should not be assigned or assumed by a higher organization or authority (O'Brien 1987a). The concern of the superintendent is not whether a parish is heeding his or her advice; but rather to believe that the "locals," knowing all the relevant details of a local situation, actually do know best how to deal with the school. If one really believes in subsidiarity, then with that belief comes the corollary that the Holy Spirit is working with and through these people.

What should the superintendent do if the pastor tells the principal to do something directly contrary to state law or federal mandate? The superintendent, as chief advisor to the pastor, has an obligation to inform the pastor of

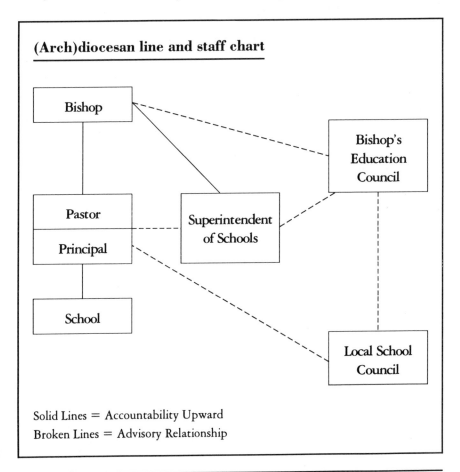

(Arch)diocesan line and staff chart

Bishop

Bishop's Education Council

Pastor

Principal

Superintendent of Schools

School

Local School Council

Solid Lines = Accountability Upward
Broken Lines = Advisory Relationship

the problem and the potential ramifications for the school. If the superintendent senses the entire diocesan system is being called into jeopardy, then he or she has the obligation to inform the bishop.

To summarize, the superintendent should not be making parish school decisions, yet the pastor ought to acknowledge the superintendent's expertise about Catholic schools in general.

It is important that the superintendent demonstrate his belief in the presence of the Holy Spirit working in the parish through the pastor and principal who are concerned about their local school situation. In a similar vein, it is important for parish personnel to respect the superintendent's vision of the totality of Catholic education in the diocese. This breadth of knowledge, which no pastor of only one parish possesses, obliges the superintendent to act in the best interest of all the schools in the diocese.

Areas of superintendent expertise

Seminary training does not equip a pastor to run a school. The bishop hires a superintendent who has been professionally prepared to lead a school system/network and to support the pastors and principals in their administration of local parish schools. Ordinarily, the daily affairs of the school are easily administered on the local level with little or no assistance. The superintendent can be of crucial assistance to the pastor and schools in such areas as federal and state guidelines, finance issues, legal concerns, expedient political action, curriculum, and research practices for schools.

The superintendent should develop a central diocesan office staffed with people who have the knowledge and experience needed by the local schools. As Catholic schools become more technically advanced with computers and e-mail, the central office must provide the expertise and advice that no individual school can possibly muster in a cost-effective way. The network of Catholic schools deserves to have experts in the superintendent's office to call on as needed.

Federal and State Mandates

No pastor should even desire to know the myriad of details about state and federal assistance programs. If a pastor were to try, he could do so at the expense of his other more important and appropriate responsibilities. Even though the pastor may be wrestling with how best to use this money in the evangelization effort of his parish school, he cannot remake state and federal programs to fit nicely into his budget. Informed personnel from the superintendent's office should help the pastor and his principal develop programs that will meet local goals and still conform with the guidelines for such programs.

Finance

Finance is one of the easiest areas in which the superintendent can provide information and advice to the pastor. The superintendent can generate non-judgmental trend comparisons of income and expenses for all the schools and inform the pastor of his school's situation in regard to these trends. Individual schools can not easily generate this critical information. These comparisons will provide insights that facilitate improvement at the local level. This job is made considerably easier if the diocese has a uniform accounting system. The trick for the superintendent is to provide ample information and then let the local school evaluate it. Such information allows local administrators and their committees to interpret the implications of these facts. For instance, if a particular school has a low plant-operating cost, that does not automatically transfer into a failure to provide proper maintenance. If instruction cost is high, that does not mean that salaries are too high or classes too small. Those evaluative judgments are best left to the local school personnel. Only in the most extreme cases should the superintendent indicate that the local situation is awry.

Such cost comparisons inevitably lead the superintendent into another area where his or her expertise can be of use, namely that of the budget. Many seemingly arcane areas of budget are the same for all the schools in a particular area, e.g., rate increases in utilities. One call to the State Public Utilities Commission will ferret out these figures, making the local budgeting effort easier. The superintendent's office can provide a valuable service by ascertaining readily available general information concerning the schools. While the super-intendent's office should not be burdened with finding figures that apply to only one location, information that applies to many institutions, e.g., Blue Cross/Blue Shield rates, can be useful and time saving. There are other offices in the diocese, e.g., finance, where this could be done. Thus some diocesan coordination is necessary to ensure that functions are not duplicated. The main point is that the superintendent's office should act when it can assist several schools and avoid duplicating local effort. Without turning the diocese into a system, the superintendent's office should be able to supply other budgetary items such as comparative tuitions and salary scales. All this information can be forwarded as pertinent knowledge without forcing local decisions or even suggesting what a particular school should do. The superintendent's office simply contributes to the local school the advantage of knowing the larger picture.

Legal Concerns

Another area where the superintendent brings expertise is in the whole legal realm as it pertains to the school. Since, in our litigious society, school legal squabbles are not unusual, strategies and procedures should be coordinated. When a legal question arises, the superintendent should know whether some other local school has faced the same problem; in this case, it is possible that no lawyer need be involved or only a local lawyer is necessary. The superintendent should be able to help sort out whether there is a precedent-setting situation. Finally, the superintendent should be able to determine whether the diocesan attorney is necessary, and who should pay the bill. If all these functions are seen by both the superintendent and the pastor/principal as advisory in nature, then the local pastor/principal should have no difficulty in seeking advice which will strengthen local autonomy.

Personnel issues: Termination of teachers is one of the most critical legal or quasi-legal areas. The United States system clearly helps defend the "poor little teacher" against the "big powerful institution" of the Church. Consequently, and especially for reasons of justice, it is wise to call on those who have expertise in justice, the laws, and schools to be certain that a good decision is made with a particular employee. The ability to have a real expert in such a situation is most valuable. What better way to strengthen a local principal's decision to terminate or not renew than to get an honest evaluation from someone at the diocesan level who is perceived as an expert in teacher evaluation?

An extension of this issue is the hiring and dismissal of the local principal. The pastor has the onus of hiring and dismissing a principal but he ordinarily does not have a sophisticated knowledge of Catholic school leadership competencies. While he may have people with expertise in his parish, very often that expertise will be in public education, which is not directly transferable to the parish school situation. The superintendent and the cadre of experts he or she gathers are in the best position to advise the pastor in this area. In conformity with personnel policies and procedures, the role of those education experts will often be advisory rather than dictatorial to the pastor.

Political Action: The question of political action should be considered in conjuction with strictly legal advice. Rarely will political action be the purview of a single school. How the schools should act in concert is again a question of coordination in which the superintendent's advice may be critical. The pastor/principal should readily seek the superintendent's advice before moving into the political arena. Political action of a State Catholic Conference needs coordination at the local school level. The superintendent is the diocesan coordinator of such political action.

Research

In the "good old days" of the '40s and '50s when sister principal gave the pastor, via the kids, a bouquet of roses on his name's day and the kids got the day off, that was a lot more than the old-fashioned church. It was an excellent way of currying the favor of the pastor. Such actions were not at all silly and perhaps, in hindsight, had little to do with name's day and a lot to do with keeping the school the darling of the pastor's eye. Many of those practices are hopefully gone in favor of more realistic and reasoned behaviors. The real question in the '90s is how the school can recognize the pastor's role and contribution.

It must be clearly seen that the school cannot take for granted that it is the darling of the pastor's eye. O'Brien's book *Mixed Messages* (1987b) makes that very clear. The cost pressure alone will make even the pastor who is the most ardent supporter of Catholic schools wince. The question then becomes how to convince the pastor of the importance and value of the Catholic school.

If there is anyone in the diocese who should make the time to read and digest the myriad of studies done on Catholic schools since Greeley's (1966) early work through the latest studies, it is the superintendent. Every superintendent needs to read *Catholic Schools Make a Difference* (Convey 1992). The next challenge is to package the research information and present it in an effective form to the pastors. A variety of methods can be tried, e.g., deanery meetings and pastors' luncheons. Bulletins to pastors are a possibility although they are already inundated with unread mail. Pastors no longer are Lone Rangers. Most of them work with a staff. Consequently, going to the parish and informing the total staff on the research is becoming an increasingly time-consuming though excellent model. To the superintendent who cries that she or he does not have time to do this, a quick glance back at the monarchical model may make more time available for what simply must be done in the light of *Mixed Messages*.

Characteristics of a pro-school pastor

The superintendent can also ease principal-pastor relations by assisting the pastor in understanding his role in relationship to the school. It is often very difficult for a principal to say to a pastor: "Let me run the school." It is often far easier for the outside expert to assist the pastor in carving out what his role in the school should be, given his own personality and the strengths and weaknesses of the principal. If the superintendent has been in the diocese for a while, she or he may also help the principal facilitate a smooth relationship with the pastor. The following ten characteristics of a pastor who is seen to be pro-school are offered to help the pastor involve himself in a positive way with the school. Keep in mind that no one pastor will ever incarnate all these characteristics. The important thing is for the pastor to develop a comfortable working style. Consistent with the message of this chapter, these ideas are given in the spirit of friendly advice for the pastor's reflection and consideration.

- The pastor in consultation with the principal attends faculty staff meetings occasionally throughout the school year and participates actively in the discussion.
- The pastor knows the entire staff, both professional and nonprofessional, by name and shows concern for their personal lives and problems.
- The pastor participates in social events involving the school staff. He initiates and finances some staff social events.
- The pastor initiates, helps plan, carries out, and participates with the staff and students in religious activities such as liturgies, para-liturgies, retreats, and sacramental programs that reflect the Catholic values of the community.
- The pastor becomes more than just verbally involved in student and school activities outside the classroom, e.g., choir, plays, and social events.
- The pastor makes a concerted effort to know the students' names in order to relate with them on a one-to-one basis.
- The pastor works to establish an image of compassion and concern for the individual welfare of the parish children and avoids the disciplinarian and authoritarian image.
- The pastor expresses to others a positive attitude toward all financial and development programs which are set up for improvement of the school. Regardless of his personal apprehension, he displays an attitude of confidence.
- The pastor encourages the children to attend Catholic high school.

- The pastor exercises the principle of subsidiarity in dealing with all school-community relations. Rather than making school-related decisions himself, he defers to those immediately in charge.
- The pastor in consultation with the principal shows concern about the physical appearance of the school building. He budgets money for the proper maintenance of the buildings. He follows through to a satisfactory solution on all maintenance problems.

Strengthening the pastor's role

Any superintendent can sit with a pastor and, being sensitive to the pastor's personality, assist him in working out his role. This works when the superintendent makes it clear to the pastor that his role is far broader than just supplying money for the school. Perhaps the most effective way to achieve all this is an annual visit to the pastor in his rectory. There is no better way to say loudly to the pastor: "You are important." The size of the diocese and the needs of the pastor will dictate frequency. Sensitive advice must be carefully crafted to fit the local situation. Participants should put aside theological differences in these discussions and the good of the school should be the goal.

It must be acknowledged that the pastor's direct link with the school is the principal. However, if we are going to choose our titles from the public school model, e.g., superintendent, instead of vicar for education or secretary to the bishop for schools, then it is logical to employ a title for the pastor out of that model. Since the bishop will want a person directly responsible to him, i.e., the superintendent, and since the pastor is the ultimate local authority, the title "local superintendent" for the pastor seems to fit. While the pastor may be viewed as a local superintendent, this should not mitigate in any way the concept of the pastor/principal team. This working relationship between the pastor and principal is somewhat analogous to the relationship between the local superintendent and principal in public school settings.

Summary

What can the pastor expect of the superintendent? The wise superintendent will make clear that he or she has read canon 519, takes it seriously, and respects its implications. He or she will make clear to the pastor the line and staff chart given earlier in this essay. He or she will make clear to the pastor that he or she genuinely believes in subsidiarity, by both word and action. The superintendent will demonstrate that he or she has a depth of information at the disposal of the pastor, ready to help him in whatever way he or she can. He or she will make clear the role of the pastor as local superintendent. He or she will make clear that the diocesan superintendent does not have a transfer of functions from the public school superintendent. Most of all the superintendent will make clear that he or she is a loyal advisor to the pastor and is there to help chiefly through advice. The superintendent will make clear to the pastor that he or she will stand by the pastor through any school crisis.

Conclusion

This essay is an attempt to understand the role of the superintendent in relation to the pastor. The basic thesis is that understanding must be sought within the traditions of the Church and not in the American public school model. The ancient tradition of the Church prior to 1870 was that of collegiality in the running of the Church. The bishops were regarded as consultors to the papacy. When the Second Vatican Council was held, there were some 2,300 bishops. Most of those bishops knew little of the American public school board, born of a different necessity on the American frontier. The bishops did not try to adopt a similar form for the Church. The Church had an older model of collegiality. Building on that model, the bishop had a number of advisors in various areas. One of these areas was education and specifically Catholic schools. The superintendent in the ecclesial situation becomes the chief advisor to the bishop in the area of Catholic schools. This essay supports the idea that every pastor is in some way a local superintendent. The superintendent is an advisor to the pastor regarding the parish school.

Reflection Questions

1. How does the *Code of Canon Law* affect the school?

2. List the differences between a network and a system of schools.

3. Discuss the concept: "Power asserted is influence denied; influence asserted is power denied."

4. Is it possible for the superintendent to take a nonauthoritative role in relation to the Catholic parochial school? Describe the circumstances that make it possible. Will it be effective?

5. How does the principle of subsidiarity apply to the schools in a diocese and in a parish?

6. Develop a line and staff chart of your diocese and its schools.

7. List the areas of expertise needed for your school. Where should this expertise be found?

8. Describe the role and title of the pastor in the parish with a school.

9. Discuss the merits of the "characteristics of the pro-school pastor" in light of your current situation. Is this description realistic? Is this list complete? What would you add or delete?

Resources

Convey, J. J. 1992. *Catholic schools make a difference*. Washington, D.C.: National Catholic Educational Association.

Coriden, J., et al., eds. 1985. *The code of Canon Law*. New York: Paulist Press.

Greeley, A. M. 1966. *The education of Catholic Americans*. Chicago: Aldine Publishing Company.

————. 1992. A modest proposal for the reform of Catholic schools. Summarized in *National congress: Catholic schools for the 21st century: Executive summary*, eds. M. Guerra, R. Haney, and R. Kealey. Washington, D.C.: National Catholic Educational Association.

Kealey, R., ed. 1989. *Reflections on the role of the Catholic school principal*. Washington, D.C.: National Catholic Education Association.

Korda, M. 1975. *Power*. New York: Random House.

Kouzes, J., and B. Posner. 1989. *The leadership challenge*. San Francisco: Jossey-Bass Publishers.

National Congress: Catholic Schools for the 21st Century. 1992a. Leadership of and on behalf of Catholic schools. In *National congress: Catholic schools for the 21st century: Executive Summary*, eds. M. Guerra, R. Haney, and R. Kealey. Washington, D.C.: National Catholic Educational Association.

————. 1992b. Political action, public policy and Catholic schools. In *National congress: Catholic schools for the 21st century: Executive Summary*, eds. M. Guerra, R. Haney, and R. Kealey. Washington, D.C.: National Catholic Educational Association.

O'Brien, J. S., ed. 1987a. *A primer on educational governance in the Catholic Church*. CACE/NABE Governance Task Force. Washington, D.C.: National Catholic Educational Association.

————. 1987b. *Mixed messages: What bishops and priests say about Catholic schools*. Washington, D.C.: National Catholic Educational Association.

Peters, T., and R. Waterman. 1982. *In search of excellence*. New York: Warner Books.

Shaughnessy, M. A. 1989. *School handbooks: Some legal considerations*. Washington, D.C.: National Catholic Educational Association.

Simon, H. 1957. *Administrative behavior*. New York: The Free Press.

Williston, W., R. Norris, D. Lotz, and R. Handy. 1958. *A history of the Christian Church*. New York: Charles Scribner's Sons.

The author, Fr. John A. Thomas, Ph.D., is pastor of St. Rose Parish in Perrysburg, Ohio.

General
Bibliography
◆◆◆

Abbott, W. M., ed. 1966. *Declaration on Christian education (Gravissimum educationis)*. In *The documents of Vatican II*, trans. Joseph Gallagher. New York: The Guild Press.

Anderson, C. S. 1982. The search for school climate: A review of the research. *Review of Educational Research* 52(3):368–420.

Bass, B. M. 1985. *Leadership and performance beyond expectations*. New York: The Free Press.

Bennett, K. P., and M. D. LeCompte. 1990. *How schools work: A sociological analysis of education*. White Plains, N.Y.: Longman.

Bennis, W. 1984. Transformation power and leadership. In *Leadership and organizational culture*, ed. T. J. Sergiovanni and J. E. Corbally, 64–71. Urbana-Champaign: University of Illinois Press.

———. 1985. *Leaders*. New York: Harper and Row.

Bennis, W. A., and B. Nanus. 1988. *Leaders*. New York: Harper and Row.

Benson, P. L., and M. J. Guerra. 1985. *Sharing the faith: The beliefs and values of Catholic high school teachers*. Washington, D.C.: National Catholic Educational Association.

Bernadin, J. 1989. Catholic schools: Opportunities and challenges. *Chicago Studies* 28(3):211–16.

Brigham, F. H. 1993. *United States Catholic elementary and secondary schools 1992–93*. Washington, D.C.: National Catholic Educational Association.

Bryk, A. S., P. B. Holland, V. E. Lee, and R. A. Carriedo. 1984. *Effective Catholic schools: An exploration*. Washington, D.C.: National Catholic Educational Association.

Bryk, A. S., V. E. Lee, and P. B. Holland. 1993. *Catholic schools and the common good*. Cambridge, Mass.: Harvard University Press.

Bryson, J. M. 1990. *Strategic planning for public and nonprofit organizations*. San Francisco: Jossey-Bass Publishers.

Buetow, H. A. 1988. *The Catholic school: Its roots, identity, and future*. New York: Crossroad Publishing Company.

Burke, R. 1984. *Elementary school finance manual*. Washington, D.C.: National Catholic Educational Association.

Burns, J. M. 1978. *Leadership*. New York: Harper and Row.

Bushman, E. M., and G. J. Sparks, eds. 1990. *The Catholic school administrator: A book of readings*. Portland, Ore.: Catholic Leadership Co.

Canon Law Society of America. 1983. *Code of canon law: Latin-English edition*. Washington, D.C.: Canon Law Society of America.

Castetter, W. B. 1986. *The personnel function in educational administration*. 4th ed. New York: MacMillan.

Catholic schools face fiscal facts. 1993. Editorial. *America* 169(18):3.

Chubb, J. E., and T. M. Moe. 1990. *Politics, markets, and America's schools.* Washington, D.C.: The Brookings Institution.

Ciriello, M. J. 1988. Teachers in Catholic school: A study of commitment. Ph.D. diss., The Catholic University of America, 1987. Abstract in *Dissertations Abstracts International* 48:8514A.

―――. 1991. *Catholic principals' survey concerning their role and the future of Catholic education in the Archdiocese of Boston.* Boston: Catholic Schools Office.

―――. 1992. *Attitudes of Catholic school administrators of the Diocese of Honolulu concerning their role and the future of Catholic education on the Islands.* Honolulu, Hawaii: Catholic School Department.

Ciriello, M. J., and J. J. Convey. 1993. Catholic higher education and diocesan school departments collaborating to strengthen leadership. *Current Issues in Catholic Higher Education* 14(1):34–39.

Clifton, D., and P. Nelson. 1992. *Soar with your strengths.* New York: Delacourte Press.

Coleman, J. 1987. *Public and private high schools: The impact of communities.* New York: Basic Books.

Coleman, J. S., and T. Hoffer. 1987. *Public and private high schools: The impact of communities.* New York: Basic Books.

Conger, J. A., and R. N. Kanungo, et al. 1988. *Charismatic leadership, the elusive factor in organizational effectiveness.* San Francisco: Jossey-Bass Publishers.

Congregation for Catholic Education. 1977. *The Catholic school.* Washington, D.C.: United States Catholic Conference.

―――. 1982. *Lay Catholics in schools: Witnesses to faith.* Boston: Daughters of St. Paul.

―――. 1988. *The religious dimension of education in a Catholic school: Guidelines for reflection and renewal.* Washington, D.C.: United States Catholic Conference.

Convey, J. J. 1992. *Catholic schools make a difference.* Washington, D.C.: National Catholic Educational Association.

Coriden, J., et al., eds. 1985. *The code of canon law.* New York: Paulist Press.

Covey, S. R. 1989. *The seven habits of highly effective people.* New York: Simon and Schuster.

―――. 1991. *Principle-centered leadership.* New York: Simon and Schuster.

Cunningham, W. G., and D. W. Gresso. 1994. *Cultural leadership: The culture of excellence in education.* Needham, Mass.: Allyn and Bacon.

De La Salle, J. B. [ca. 1730] 1975. *Meditations for the time of retreat.* Trans. A. Loes. Romeoville, Ill.: Christian Brothers Conference.

De Pree, M. 1989. *Leadership is an art.* New York: Doubleday.

―――. 1992. *Leadership jazz.* New York: Doubleday.

Deal, T. E. 1987. The culture of schools. In *Leadership: Examining the elusive, 1987 Yearbook*, 3–15. Alexandria, Va.: Association for Supervision and Curriculum Development.

Deal, T. E., and A. A. Kennedy. 1983. Culture and school performance. *Educational Leadership* 40(5):14–15.

Deal, T. E., and K. D. Peterson. 1990. *The principal's role in shaping school culture.* Washington, D.C.: United States Department of Education.

Donaldson, F. 1991. *Catholic school publications: Unifying the image.* Washington, D.C.: National Catholic Educational Association.

Drahmann, T., and A. Stenger. 1989. *The Catholic school principal: An outline for action.* Revised. Washington, D.C.: National Catholic Educational Association.

Droel, W. 1989. *The spirituality of work: Teachers.* Chicago: National Center for the Laity.

Edmonds, R. R. 1979. Effective schools for the urban poor. *Educational Leadership* 37(2):15–27.

Elias, J. 1989. *Moral education: Secular and religious.* Malabar, Fla.: R. E. Krieger Publishers.

Epstein, J. L. 1987. Toward a theory of family-school connections: Teachers practices and parent involvement across school years. In *Social intervention: Potential and constraints*, ed. D. Hurrelmann, F. Kaufmann, and F. Losel. New York: de Grutra Press.

Fiedler, F. E. 1964. A contingency model of leadership effectiveness. In *Advances in experimental social psychology*, ed. L. Berkowitz. New York: Academic Press.

Ford, E. R. 1992. Faith alive: A wake-up call. *Today's Catholic Teacher* 25(7):50–54.

French, J. R., and B. Raven. 1959. The bases of social power. In *Studies in social power*, ed. D. Cartwright. Ann Arbor, Mich.: Institute for Social Research.

Fullan, M. G. 1991. *The new meaning of educational change.* New York: Teacher's College.

Galton, F. 1870. *Hereditary genius.* New York: Appleton.

Gary, B. S. 1986. *Seeking foundation grants.* Washington, D.C.: National Catholic Educational Association.

Gilbert, J. 1983. *Pastor as shepherd of the school community.* Washington, D.C.: National Catholic Educational Association.

Glatthorn, A. A. 1987. *Curriculum renewal.* Alexandria, Va.: Association for Supervision and Curriculum Development.

Gonser, Gerber, Tinker, and Stuhr. 1988. *On development.* Chicago.

Grant, M. A., and T. C. Hunt. 1992. *Catholic school education in the United States.* New York: Garland Publishing.

Greeley, A. M. 1966. *The education of Catholic Americans.* Chicago: Aldine Publishing Company.

———. 1992. A modest proposal for the reform of catholic schools. Summarized in *National Congress: Catholic Schools for the 21st: Executive Summary*, eds. M. Guerra, R. Haney, and R. Kealey. Washington, D.C.: National Catholic Educational Association.

Guerra, M. J. 1993. *Dollars and sense: Catholic high schools and their finances 1992.* Washington, D.C.: National Catholic Educational Association.

Guerra, M., R. Haney, and R. Kealey, eds. 1992. *National congress: Catholic schools for the 21st century: Executive summary.* Washington, D.C.: National Catholic Educational Association.

Hanlon, J. M. 1973. *Theory, practice and education*. Fond du Lac, Wis.: Marian College Press.

Harris, J. C. 1992. Is the American Catholic Church getting out of the elementary school business? *Chicago Studies* 31(1):81–92.

———. 1994. Catholics can too afford schools. *America* 170(8):22–24.

Heft, J. 1991. Catholic identity and the Church. In *What makes a Catholic school Catholic?*, ed. F. D. Kelly, 14–21. Washington, D.C.: National Catholic Educational Association.

Helm, C. M. 1989. Cultural and symbolic leadership in Catholic elementary schools: An ethnographic study. Ph.D. diss., The Catholic University of America, Washington, D.C.

Hersey, P., and K. H. Blanchard. 1977. *The management of organizational behavior*. 3d ed. Englewood Cliffs, N.J.: Prentice-Hall.

———. 1984. *The management of organizational behavior*. 4th ed. Englewood Cliffs, N.J.: Prentice Hall.

Hind, J. F. 1989. *The heart and soul of effective management: A Christian approach to managing and motivating people*. Wheaton, Ill.: Victor Books.

Hocevar, R. 1991. Catholic school governance. In *Catholic school governance and finance*. Washington, D.C.: National Catholic Educational Association.

Hollander, E. P. 1985. Leadership and power. In *Handbook of social psychology*. Vol. II, *Special fields and applications*, ed. E. Aronson, 3d ed., 485–537. New York: Random House.

House, R. J. 1971. A path goal theory of leader effectiveness. *Administrative Science Quarterly* 16: 321–39.

———. 1977. A 1976 theory of charismatic leadership. In *Leadership: The cutting edge*, ed. J. G. Hunt and L. L. Larson, 189–207. Carbondale: Southern Illinois University Press.

John Paul II. 1982. *On the family (Familiaris consortio)*. Washington, D.C.: United States Catholic Conference.

———. 1987. The Catholic school of the '80s. *Origins* 17(17).

Joyce, B., and B. Showers. 1995. Student achievement through staff development: Fundamentals of school renewal. White Plains, N.Y.: Longman.

Katz, R. L. 1955. Skills of an effective administrator. *Harvard Business Review* January-February:33–42.

Kealey, R., ed. 1989a. *Reflections on the role of the Catholic school principal*. Washington, D.C.: National Catholic Education Association.

———. 1989b. The unique dimension of the Catholic school. *Momentum* 20(1):29.

———. 1992. *United States Catholic elementary schools and their finances 1991*. Washington, D.C.: National Catholic Educational Association.

Kellerman, B., ed. 1984. *Leadership: Multidisciplinary perspectives*. Englewood Cliffs, N.J.: Prentice-Hall.

Kelly, F. D., ed. 1991. *What makes a Catholic school Catholic?* Washington, D.C.: National Catholic Educational Association.

Konzen J. 1991. *The role of the principal in development*. Washington, D.C.: National Catholic Educational Association.

Korda, M. 1975. *Power*. New York: Random House.

Kouzes, J., and B. Posner. 1989. *The leadership challenge*. San Francisco: Jossey-Bass Publishers.

La Riviere, A. 1993. *The development council: Cornerstone for success*. Washington, D.C.: National Catholic Educational Association.

Larranaga, R. 1990. *Calling it a day: Daily meditations for workaholics*. San Francisco: Harper and Row.

Larson, C. E., and F. M. LaFasto. 1991. *Teamwork*. Newbury Park, Calif.: Sage Publications.

Leak, L., B. McKay, P. Splain, P. Walker, and C. Held. 1990. *Professional development resource book for school principals*. College Park, Md.: University of Maryland Printing Service.

Leo XIII. 1887, 1979. Common duties and interests. In *Education: Papal teachings*, by the Benedictine Monks of Solesemes, trans. A. Robeschini. Boston: Daughters of St. Paul.

Lickona, T. 1991. *Educating for character*. New York: Bantam Books.

Maeroff, G. I. 1993. Team building. *Phi Delta Kappan* 74(7):512–19.

Mann, F. C. 1965. Toward an understanding of the leadership role in formal organization. In *Leadership and productivity*, ed. R. Dubin, G. C. Homans, F. C. Mann, and D. C. Miller. San Francisco: Chandler.

Mann, W. E. 1991. *The Lasallian school: Where teachers assist parents in the education and formation of children*. Narragansett, R.I.: Brothers of the Christian Schools, Long Island-New England Province, Inc.

McBride, A. A. 1981. *The Christian formation of Catholic educators, A CACE monograph*. Washington, D.C.: National Catholic Educational Association.

McCelland, D. 1970. The two faces of power. *Journal of International Affairs* 24(1):29–47.

————. 1975. *Power: The inner experience*. New York: Irvington.

McCormick, M. T. 1994. Close, but no cigar. *America* 170(8):24–26.

McDermott, E. 1985. Distinctive qualities of the Catholic school. In *NCEA Keynote Series No. 1*. Washington, D.C.: National Catholic Educational Association.

McGhee, C. 1993. Barefoot prophets. *Momentum* 24(3):55.

Miner, J. B. 1978. Twenty years of research on role motivation theory of managerial effectiveness. *Personnel Psychology* 31:739–60.

Monetti-Souply, M. 1990. *A year-round recruitment and retention plan*. Washington, D.C.: National Catholic Educational Association.

National Catholic Educational Association. 1982. *Code of ethics for the Catholic school teacher*. Washington, D.C.

National Congress: Catholic Schools for the 21st Century. 1992a. Leadership of and on behalf of Catholic schools. In *National congress: Catholic schools for the 21st century: Executive Summary*, eds. M. Guerra, R. Haney, and R. Kealey. Washington, D.C.: National Catholic Educational Association.

————. 1992b. Political action, public policy and Catholic schools. In *National congress: Catholic schools for the 21st century: Executive Summary*, eds. M. Guerra, R. Haney, and R. Kealey. Washington, D.C.: National Catholic Educational Association.

National Conference of Catholic Bishops. 1972. *To teach as Jesus did: A pastoral message on Catholic education*. Washington, D.C.: United States Catholic Conference.

————. 1979. *Sharing the light of faith: National catechetical directory for Catholics of the United States*. Washington, D.C.: United States Catholic Conference.

————. 1990. *In support of Catholic elementary and secondary schools*. Washington, D.C.: United States Catholic Conference.

Neuman, M. 1987. Modern media and the religious sense of community. *Review for Religious* 46(2):195–201.

————. 1992. Pastoral leadership beyond the managerial. *Review for Religious* 51(4):585–94.

Nouwen, H. 1989. *In the name of Jesus: Reflections on Christian leadership*. New York: Crossroad Publishing Company.

Nucci, L., ed. 1989. *Moral development and character education*. Berkeley, Calif.: McCutchan Publisher.

O'Brien, J. S., ed. 1987a. *A primer on educational governance in the Catholic Church*. CACE/NABE Governance Task Force. Washington, D.C.: National Catholic Educational Association.

————. 1987b. *Mixed messages: What bishops and priests say about Catholic schools*. Washington, D.C.: National Catholic Educational Association.

O'Malley, W. J. 1991. Evangelizing the unconverted. In *What makes a Catholic school Catholic?*, ed. F. D. Kelly, 3–9. Washington, D.C.: National Catholic Educational Association.

Oldenburg, R. L. 1991. *Conducting the phonathon*. Washington, D.C.: National Catholic Educational Association.

Peters, T., and R. Waterman. 1982. *In search of excellence*. New York: Warner Books.

Peterson, J. 1990. *How to hire a development officer: From defining needs to ensuring successful performance*. Washington, D.C.: National Catholic Educational Association.

Pistone, A. J. 1987. Nourishing the faith life of the teacher. *Momentum* 18(1):47.

Pius IX. 1929, 1979. Education of the redeemed man. In *Education: Papal teachings*, by the Benedictine Monks of Solesemes, trans. A. Robeschini. Boston: Daughters of St. Paul.

Pius XI. 1929. *On the Christian education of youth*. Boston: Daughters of St. Paul.

Purkey, S., and M. S. Smith. 1982. Synthesis of research on effective schools. *Educational Leadership* 40(3):64–69.

Ramsey, D. A. 1991. *Empowering leaders*. Kansas City: Sheed and Ward.

Reid, D. G., ed. 1990. *Dictionary of Christianity in America*. Downers Grove, Ill.: Intervarsity Press.

Ristau, K. 1991. The challenge to provide leadership within Catholic schools. In *Leadership of on behalf of Catholic schools*. Washington, D.C.: National Catholic Educational Association.

Roberts, W. 1985. *Leadership secrets of Attila the Hun*. New York: Warner Books.

Schein, E. 1992. *Organizational culture and leadership*. 2d ed. San Francisco: Jossey-Bass Publishers.

Schillebeeckx, E. 1981. *Ministry, leadership in the community of Jesus Christ*. New York: Crossroad Publishing Company.

Scholtes, P. 1989. *The team handbook*. Madison, Wis.: Joiner Associates.

Secretan, L. H. K. 1993. *Managerial moxie*. Rocklin, Calif.: Prima Publishing.

Sergiovanni, T. J. 1984. Leadership and excellence in schooling. *Educational Leadership* 41(5):4–13.

———. 1987. *The principalship: A reflective practice perspective*. Boston: Allyn and Bacon.

———. 1990. *Value-added leadership: How to get extraordinary performance in schools*. San Diego: Harcourt, Brace, Jovanovich Publishers.

———. 1992. *Moral leadership: Getting to the heart of school improvement*. San Francisco: Jossey-Bass Publishers.

Sergiovanni, T. J., and J. E. Corbally. 1986. *Leadership and organizational culture*. Chicago: University of Illinois Press.

Shaughnessy, M. A. 1989. *School handbooks: Some legal considerations*. Washington, D.C.: National Catholic Educational Association.

Sheehan, L. 1990. *Building better boards*. Washington, D.C.: National Catholic Educational Association.

———. 1991. Governance. In *Catholic school governance and finance*. Washington, D.C.: National Catholic Educational Association.

Simon, H. 1957. *Administrative behavior*. New York: The Free Press.

SRI Gallup. 1990. Themes of the Catholic school principal. In *The Catholic school principal perceiver: Concurrent validity report*. Lincoln, Neb.: Human Resources for Ministry Institute.

———. 1991. Themes of the Catholic school teacher. In *The Catholic school principal perceiver: Concurrent validity report*. Lincoln, Neb.: Human Resources for Ministry Institute.

Stangl, A. 1990. *The one-person development office*. Washington, D.C.: National Catholic Educational Association.

Stogdill, R. M. 1974. *Handbook of leadership: A survey of theory and research*. New York: The Free Press.

Stone, S. C. 1987. *Strategic planning for independent schools*. Boston: National Association of Independent Schools.

———. 1993. *Shaping strategy: Independent school planning in the '90s*. Boston: National Association of Independent Schools.

Tagiuri, R. 1968. The concept of organizational climate. In *Organizational climate: Exploration of a concept*, ed. R. Tagiuri and G. H. Litwin. Boston: Harvard University, Division of Research, Graduate School of Business Administration.

Tarr, H. C. 1990a. *Teacher values and commitment orientations*. A Report to the Archdiocese of Boston Strategic Planning Study for Schools, October 29, 1990. Washington, D.C.: The Catholic University of America.

————. 1990b. *Teacher satisfaction, attitudes and attributions.* A Report for the Archdiocese of Boston Strategic Planning Study for Schools, December 21, 1990. Washington, D.C.: The Catholic University of America.

Tarr, H. C., M. J. Ciriello, and J. J. Convey. 1993. Commitment and satisfaction among parochial school teachers: Findings from Catholic education. *Journal of Research on Christian Education* 2(1):41–63.

Tedesco, J. 1991. *Catholic schools and volunteers: A planned involvement.* Washington, D.C.: National Catholic Educational Association.

Thomas, J. A., and B. Davis. 1989. The principal as part of the pastoral team. In *Reflections on the role of the Catholic school principal,* ed. R. Kealey. Washington, D.C.: National Catholic Educational Association.

Thompson, L. A., and J. A. Flynn. 1988. *Effective funding of Catholic schools.* Kansas City, Mo.: Sheed and Ward.

Tracy, M. 1990. *Steps in direct solicitation: Preparation, presentation, and follow-up.* Washington, D.C.: National Catholic Educational Association.

Traviss, M. P. 1985. *Student moral development in the Catholic school.* Washington, D.C.: National Catholic Educational Association.

United States Department of Education. 1983. *A nation at risk: The imperative for educational reform.* Washington, D.C.

Vaill, P. B. 1984. The purposing of high-performing systems. In *Leadership and organizational culture,* ed. T. J. Sergiovanni and J. E. Corbally, 85–104. Urbana: University of Illinois Press.

Vroom, V. H., and P. W. Yetton. 1973. *Leadership and decision-making.* Pittsburgh: University of Pittsburgh Press.

Weakland, R. G. 1994. Foreword in *From the heart of the American Church,* by D. J. O'Brien. Maryknoll, N.Y.: Orbis Books.

Weber, M. 1947. *The theory of social and economic organization.* New York: Oxford University Press.

Whyte, W. F. 1969. *Organizational behavior: Theory and applications.* Homewood, Ill.: Irwin.

Williston, W., R. Norris, D. Lotz, and R. Handy. 1958. *A history of the Christian Church.* New York: Charles Scribner's Sons.

Woodward, E. 1987. *Poets, prophets & pragmatists: A new challenge to religious life.* Notre Dame, Ind.: Ave Maria Press.

Yeager, R. J., P. L. Benson, M. J. Guerra, and B.V. Manno. 1985. *The Catholic high school: A national portrait.* Washington, D.C.: National Catholic Educational Association.

Yukl, G. A. 1981. *Leadership in organizations.* Englewood Cliffs, N.J.: Prentice-Hall, Inc.

Yukl, G. A., and W. Nemeroff. 1979. Identification and measurement of specific categories of leadership behavior: A progress report. In *Crosscurrents in leadership,* ed. J. G. Hunt and L. L. Larson. Cardondale: Southern Illinios University Press.